HISTORY'S MYSTERIES

Priyankee Saikia is an author from Guwahati, Assam and this is her first book. She has a Master's degree in English Literature from the University of Delhi. She discovered her love for writing at the age of six, when she began jotting down her first few poems. Since then, she has written for a number of regional newspapers, magazines and online blogs, besides running her college magazine and various newsletters.

A former journalist and copywriter, today she is a digital marketer by profession. She continues to dabble in writing during her free time and hopes to publish fiction one day. As a mother of an inquisitive four-year-old, Priyankee loves telling stories to her daughter and dreams of travelling the world with her.

In a perfect universe, the author would love nothing more than a roomful of books and all the time in the world to read them.

HISTORY'S MYSTERIES

51 Intriguing Secrets of the Past

PRIYANKEE SAIKIA

RUPA

Published by
Rupa Publications India Pvt. Ltd 2021
7/16, Ansari Road, Daryaganj
New Delhi 110002

Sales Centres:
Allahabad Bengaluru Chennai
Hyderabad Jaipur Kathmandu
Kolkata Mumbai

Copyright © Priyankee Saikia 2021

The views and opinions expressed in this book are the author's own and the facts are as reported by her which have been verified to the extent possible, and the publishers are not in any way liable for the same.

All rights reserved.

No part of this publication may be reproduced, transmitted, or stored in a retrieval system, in any form or by any means, electronic, mechanical, photocopying, recording or otherwise, without the prior permission of the publisher.

ISBN: 978-93-89967-94-4

First impression 2021

10 9 8 7 6 5 4 3 2 1

The moral right of the author has been asserted.

This book is sold subject to the condition that it shall not, by way of trade or otherwise, be lent, resold, hired out, or otherwise circulated, without the publisher's prior consent, in any form of binding or cover other than that in which it is published.

For Zoe
May you never lose your sense of curiosity and wonder

Contents

Introduction ix

NATURE'S RIDDLES

1. How Did Dinosaurs Become Extinct? 2
2. Do Aliens Exist? 6
3. Why Are There No Other Human Species Alive? 10
4. What Is the Taos Hum? 14
5. Is the Bigfoot Real? 18
6. Is the Yeti Real? 21
7. Is the Loch Ness Monster Real? 25

ANCIENT CIVILIZATIONS

8. What Really Happened to the Mayans? 30
9. The Mystery of Stonehenge 34
10. What Happened to the Lost City of Atlantis? 38
11. Deciphering the Indus Valley Script 42
12. The Mystery Behind the Statues of Easter Island 47
13. Why Is the Rosetta Stone Key to Understanding Ancient Egypt? 51
14. The Mystery Behind the Nazca Lines of Peru 55
15. The Predictions of Nostradamus 59

CURIOUS ARTEFACTS

16. The Shroud of Turin 64
17. What Are the Dead Sea Scrolls? 69
18. The Voynich Manuscript 73
19. The San Bernado Mummies 77
20. The Antikythera Mechanism 80
21. The Aluminium Wedge of Aiud 84
22. The Bog Bodies of Northern Europe 87

DEATHS AND DISAPPEARANCES

23. Did Netaji Subhas Chandra Bose Really Die in a Plane Crash? 92
24. Where is the Final Resting Place of Razia Sultana? 98

25. The Lost Tomb of Cleopatra	102
26. The Disappearance of Amelia Earhart	106
27. The Disappearance of Agatha Christie	111

HISTORY'S TREASURES

28. Who Stole the Irish Crown Jewels?	116
29. The Missing Peacock Throne	120
30. The Legend of the Missing Nazi Gold	124

MYSTERIOUS PLACES

31. What Happened in the Cursed Village of Kuldhara?	128
32. Who Destroyed the Library of Alexandria?	131
33. Why Is No One Allowed on North Sentinel Island?	135
34. The Tragic Mystery of Malcha Mahal	139
35. Is Bhangarh Fort Really Haunted?	142
36. The Mystery Behind the Georgia Guidestones	145
37. The Winchester Mystery House	148

SUPERNATURAL ELEMENTS

38. Salem Witch Trials	152
39. Are Vampires Real?	155

STRANGE OCCURRENCES

40. What Caused the Dancing Plague of 1518?	160
41. What Caused the Tunguska Event?	163
42. What Happened to the Lost Colony of Ronoake?	167
43. What Happened to the *Mary Celeste*?	170
44. What Happened to the SS *Ourang Medan*?	174
45. Who Committed the Nepalese Royal Massacre?	177

UNKNOWN ENTITIES

46. Who Were the Nine Unknown Men?	182
47. Who Was Jack the Ripper?	185
48. Who Was Lucy the Australopithecus?	189
49. Who Were the Vikings?	192
50. Who Was the Zodiac Killer?	196
51. The Curious Mystery of the Electric Girl	200

Acknowledgements	203

Introduction

*'If there were no mystery left to explore,
life would get rather dull, wouldn't it?'*

—Sidney Buchman

What happens to the sun at night? Where do babies come from? If there are so many poor people, why don't governments just print more currency and distribute it among everyone?

These were the mysteries that I innocently wondered about as a child—each mystery progressing in complexity as I got older. As children, we are naturally so inquisitive that we have a question for everything: so much to explore, so many riddles to solve!

If one nurtures a child's curiosity till they get old enough to read, they realize there is an entire world of exciting mysteries to dive into. History is littered with strange events, legendary places, interesting people and puzzling things that can hold a curious mind in thrall.

There are mysteries from millions of years ago and ones that we continue to find answers to, thanks to new scientific developments and discoveries. While a lot of them have been solved, there are others, the truth of which we might never know. And yet, the exploration of all these mysteries—scattered over space and time—are a delight for adventurous minds, both young and adult alike.

History's Mysteries is an attempt to encapsulate 51 of the most intriguing secrets of the past.

When it comes to mysteries, there is no greater place to start than nature itself. The biggest animals ever to walk on Earth disappeared 65 million years ago. How? From the extinction of dinosaurs and other pre-human species, to the question of the existence of alien life, mythical creatures such as the Bigfoot, the Yeti and the Loch Ness Monster, as well as strange natural phenomenon like the Taos Hum, Mother Nature has a lot of enigmas to stir our imagination.

Strange monuments and remnants of history—such as the Stonehenge, Easter Island statues and the Nazca Lines of Peru—are sure to rouse your curiosity. Go around the world and you will come across a multitude of curious objects with interesting stories. These include the shroud in which Jesus Christ was apparently buried, artefacts such as the Antikythera Mechanism and Aluminium Wedge of Aiud, claimed to have been the work of extra-terrestrial beings (aliens, if you will), and puzzling documents such as the Voynich Manuscript and the Dead Sea Scrolls. And some of the truly shocking ones are bog bodies and mummies—human bodies preserved by nature and ancient civilizations in the strangest manner!

While these are fascinating objects, there are other equally awe-inspiring and even legendary items that have gone missing or have been stolen—and are forever lost. All that is left are stories of whodunnit. In this book, you will discover the glory that was the Peacock Throne, the lost gold of the Nazis and the Irish Crown Jewels.

Speaking of disappearances, it would be a crime to not delve into the vanishings of famed historical figures. From the famous female aviator Amelia Earhart to the crime fiction maestro Agatha Christie to the iconic Indian freedom fighter Subhash Chandra Bose, the mysteries surrounding their deaths are the stuff of legend. And then there are royal figures such as Razia Sultana and the famous Egyptian queen Cleopatra—whose tombs (or the lack of them!) continue to hound historians and archaeologists.

While these are famous people whose lives we know about, there are others whose identities continue to elude us. From the Nine Unknown Men to the entire race of Vikings, there is so much we don't know. And then there are the infamous serial killers such as Jack the Ripper and the Zodiac Killer. They say women are mysterious creatures. In this book, you will be introduced to Lucy, who is not even a human, and Angelique Cottin, who could have been a real-life member of the X-Men.

From secret societies and the apocalypse to stories of murder and mayhem, strange mysteries are also attached to historical places that are filled to the brim with fascinating tales. Read about these curious places from Bhangarh in India to the Winchester Mystery House in the US and experience the feeling of half-wonder, half-fear! Then there are also curious places you can never visit—the legendary library of Alexandria, which was unfortunately destroyed, and the North Sentinelese Island, where you'd be a fool to visit if you do not want to be murdered by hostile indigenous tribes!

You cannot talk about the riddles of the past and not be introduced to the strangest occurrences in history. There are some astounding mysteries of the sea—the disappearance of the crew of the *Mary Celeste* and the death of those on *SS Ourang Medan*. There was a plague that struck Europe in the middle ages that caused the victims to dance!

An entire colony of early English settlers went missing in America. A strange explosion in Russia flattened the forests for thousands of kilometres. The entire royal family of Nepal and a number of their relatives were gunned down one evening—while the identity of the perpetrator is still a matter of debate.

Are vampires real? The answer may surprise you. Are witches real? The executions of so-called witches in Salem will shock you. History is filled with such stories that walk the fine line between myth and reality—and at the end of the day, after all the facts are laid out for you to see, the truth of each is still a subjective matter.

NATURE'S RIDDLES

1
How Did Dinosaurs Become Extinct?

'Biological diversity is messy. It walks, it crawls, it swims, it swoops, it buzzes. But extinction is silent, and it has no voice other than our own.'

—Paul Hawken

Do you know what the biggest animal that walks on earth at this moment is? It's the African bush elephant. It can grow up to 13 feet tall and weigh more than 10 tonnes. Now let's go millions of years back in history—starting sometime around 240 million years ago and ending 65 million years ago.

Do you know how much the biggest animal from that period weighed? Up to 100 tonnes! Its height reached up to 115 feet. Yes, it was a dinosaur—the Argentinosaurus huinculensis, to be exact. If you have watched the Jurassic Park movies, you would appreciate just how big, varied and scary these animals used to be. According to palaeontologists—scientists who study dinosaurs—there were over 700 species of them that roamed the planet. They walked the land, they surveyed the deep sea and they even flew in the skies.

And then something happened, something mysterious and so destructive, that almost all the dinosaurs died after having lived and

> **DON'T JUDGE A BOOK BY ITS COVER, OR A DINOSAUR BY ITS SIZE**
>
> Even though dinosaurs seem big-toothed, sharp-clawed, menacing beasts to us, 65 per cent of all species were actually gentle herbivores. Only 35 per cent were carnivores. And not all of them were giants either. Most of them were actually small-sized, the tiniest among them being *Anchiornis huxleyi* at 160 grams in weight and 15 inches in length!

evolved for 160 million years. What was it? Scientists have a number of theories on what might possibly be one of the oldest mysteries of history.

Theory #1: Egg Hunt

How do you like to eat your eggs? Boiled? Omelette? Sunny side up? Well, animals can just eat them raw. In fact, that's what scientists earlier believed happened to the dinosaurs. Smaller animals kept stealing and eating their eggs so much that pretty soon their population could not be sustained and they died off.

Theory #2: Pea Brains

Have you noticed how all bullies are big in size, but don't seem to be very intelligent? That's another theory about the dinosaurs. Scientists believed that their small brains could not operate their big bodies anymore and thus they died out.

Theory #3: Plagues and Starvation

Some scientists believe that a great plague might have swept across the planet, killing off the dinosaurs and other animals too. Others talk of how the giant dinosaurs—most of them being plant eaters—must have had massive appetites and stripped their habitations clean of food over time, leading to starvation and later, death.

Theory #4: Climate Change

These majestic creatures thrived in a climate that was perfect for them: humid, dense and tropical. However, studies have shown that at the time the dinosaurs starting dying off, the planet was actually starting to get cooler and the oceans colder. This was called

> **BEEN THERE, DONE THAT!**
>
> If you thought that this was the worst phase our planet has been through, you're wrong. There was a worse, and bigger, destructive era 252 million years ago called the Great Dying. 90 per cent of the world's entire species was wiped out—this period was also called the Permian-Triassic Extinction. Acid rains, mercury release and now global warming have been cited as the reasons.

the late Mesozoic Era, when the North and South Poles started forming ice due to the fall in temperature. Being cold-blooded creatures, they would not have been able to survive the cold.

However, other cold-blooded animals such as crocodiles survived this. Besides, such a transformation of the climate is not sudden, and takes thousands of years, in which time the dinosaurs could have adapted to the cooler temperatures. Yet it was a theory that seemed most believable for many years.

Theory #5: Vicious Volcanoes

One of the scariest natural phenomena has to be volcanic eruptions. With their oozy red-hot lava gushing out of the earth's belly, they are known to have destroyed cities and killed hundreds of thousands of people. In fact, a giant volcano, more than 65 million years ago in India, is said to have effected global climate change that threatened the survival of dinosaurs. The lava piled up over two kilometres thick over an area of 2.6 million square kilometres.

Theory #6: Attack of the Asteroid

The first time an 'outer space' theory was put forward was in 1956, but it was dismissed for lack of evidence as well as not being able to explain why other animals survived it. The world had to wait till the 1980s to realize that the evidence was there all along. And it were two scientists—father and son duo, Luis and Walter Alvarez—who discovered it. The evidence was a layer of iridium—an element found mostly in space.

When the Alvarez duo found the centimetre-thick layer in clay in Italy from a thin band of rock that marked the extinction of dinosaurs around 65 million years ago (called the KT boundary), it was a milestone achieved in the field of palaeontology. Soon enough, scientists from different parts of the world began noting the layer of iridium. This proved that some outer space body must have collided with the earth, which caused the element to spread all over the planet.

However, if the collision was so big that it affected the entire planet, where is the evidence? The answer was found soon enough, just 10 years later, in fact. The Chicxulub Crater, which is believed to have been the spot where the collision occurred, was discovered in a peninsula of Mexico. It is 177 kilometres in diameter. Scientists have calculated that the asteroid or meteor that struck it was anything between 10 to 15 kilometres in diameter.

Racing towards the earth at an earth-shattering speed of 64,000 kilometre per hour, it would have had a massive impact. It is believed that the energy released would be more than that of millions and millions of nuclear bombs! Earthquakes, volcanoes, tsunamis, wildfires and a worldwide destruction would have left the planet struggling to survive for years. The soot itself is believed to have been around 70 billion metric tons in weight! The debris would have blocked sunlight for the longest time, cold and darkness would have enveloped the earth, killing plants at first, then herbivores and then, finally, the carnivores.

The ones to survive would have been small animals that could have burrowed in the ground and scavenged for food. Over half of the world's species would have been destroyed. Yet most mammals, some amphibians and reptiles remained—as did birds.

THE BIG REVEAL...OR NOT!

So, was it the final theory that was correct? Interestingly, iridium is also found in the earth's core—which could have spouted out with lava—so it is difficult to ascertain whether it was the meteor attack or the volcanic eruption that caused this mysterious extinction, or if it was both. Others believe that the impact of the meteor must have caused the massive volcano to erupt—although they are quite far from each other. In fact, there are scientists who believe that it was not either or both, but a combination of numerous factors including climate change that collectively wiped off the most majestic animals from our planet.

Scientists have confessed that the more information they are able to dig out about this mysterious era, the less they are convinced about any one particular theory. Perhaps that's what makes this one of the most mystifying chapters in the history of the planet.

2

Do Aliens Exist?

> *'If aliens visit us, the outcome would be much as when Columbus landed in America, which didn't turn out well for the Native Americans.'*
>
> —Stephen Hawking

The idea that we are all alone on this tiny blue planet in the corner of a galaxy in an inconceivably vast space is both unsettling and more than just a little unbelievable. As far as imagination goes, pop culture has given us entire universes of alien creatures that have defined genres such as science fiction and space fiction.

But how much truth is there in these depictions? Is there intelligent life out there elsewhere in this universe? Do they know we exist? Are they trying to communicate with us? This is and will be one of the most enduring mysteries of history, and definitely the most exciting one to be solved, if ever it is solved.

FROM AN IDEA TO A GOAL

The idea that life beyond earth may exist has been around for centuries. In fact, ancient scriptures of Jainism and even the Quran mentions cosmic pluralism—the idea that there are multiple worlds beyond our planet on which living beings exist, just like us. However, this idea gained momentum only after the telescope was invented and people realized that Earth is just one planet in an entire universe of countless planets. In the eighteenth and nineteenth centuries, it was believed that alien life existed within our solar system, particularly on Mars.

Come twentieth century, UFO sightings—and even apparent close encounters and abductions—became more frequent than ever before, most of them possible hoaxes or mistakes. With new technology and scientific advancement, space exploration became a reality in 1957, with the launch of Sputnik 1, and this has ushered in a new era of the search for alien life.

SETI AND THE SEARCH

The search for extra-terrestrial intelligence (SETI) has been going on since the invention of the radio in the early twentieth century, and today there are well-funded programmes such as the Breakthrough Initiatives, boasting names such as Mark Zuckerberg, which aim to send out messages to possible intelligent beings out there in space.

> **THE WOW! SIGNAL**
>
> On 15 August 1977, the Ohio State SETI programme recorded a surprisingly strong signal received by its telescope from outer space. Project volunteer Jerry Ehman printed it out, circled the signal, and wrote 'Wow!' on a corner. It has since been called the Wow! signal and is believed to have been sent by an extra-terrestrial source. Although it was never detected again, and the SETI Institute does not recognize it as an alien message, details about the exact location of the signal have never been made public.

Just like parapsychology (the study of paranormal and psychic phenomena) is not considered real science, SETI too is given a similar treatment among the scientific community of astronomy.

UFOs OVER HISTORY

History records the sighting of unidentified flying objects not just from hundreds of years ago, but thousands. The earliest ones date back to 1440 BC Egypt, when 'fiery discs' were reported to have been sighted floating in the skies. There have been numerous such sightings, even close encounters. One of them was in early 1803 on the Eastern shore of Japan, where fishermen examined a vessel drifting in shallow waters and reported communicating with a beautiful young woman with red and white hair and strange clothes, holding a square box she wouldn't allow anyone to touch and speaking a language they did not understand. While critics call it folklore, UFO believers consider it a close encounter of the third kind.

Such sightings of strange objects or lights in the sky have continued throughout history—retold in many movies and TV shows such as *Roswell* and *The Fourth Kind*. Even US President Jimmy Carter is known to have sighted something similar in 1969. Your author herself remembers seeing a strange flying object with blinking colourful lights up in the sky one wintry evening in the early 2010s in Delhi!

CONSPIRACY THEORIES

The little blue/green men, the big glassy eyes, the knobby-fingered hands, the beams and the spaceships, the abductions and the probes—popular fiction has more or less given us an exact idea of what extra-terrestrial encounters would look and feel like. Alien abductions have been reported throughout history, the first widely publicized one being that of a married couple—Barney and Betty Hill—in New Hampshire, US, in 1961. Both husband and wife shared vivid descriptions of encountering aliens, being taken to their spaceship and examined, and then being allowed to leave.

> ### THE SECRET BEHIND AREA 51
> Alien adventures and the US go hand-in-hand, not just in movies, but seemingly in real life as well. No one knows what work is carried out in the mysterious US Air Force facility called Area 51. But people who have worked there have apparently spoken of working on extra-terrestrial spacecrafts, alien viruses, and even alongside actual aliens, especially one called J-Rod! However, till date, the US government maintains that there is no evidence about life beyond planet Earth. Interesting, isn't it?

THE ROSWELL UFO INCIDENT

Undoubtedly, the most famous UFO incident allegedly is the one in Roswell in New Mexico in the US. In mid-1947, a wreckage was discovered by a local that included smoky grey rubber strips, tinfoil, tough paper and sticks. Some days later, a hexagonal disc was also discovered. The military went to collect all of these and informed that they were part of a crashed weather balloon, which was later revealed to be a nuclear testing balloon. However, ufologists since then have been very vocal about how this is a huge government cover-up, and the debris actually belong to a crashed spaceship.

Although this incident did not get much attention immediately in the 30-odd years since it happened, it became a major topic of discussion and debate in the 1970s—leading to a spurt in movies, TV shows, books and other platforms—setting it as one of the most iconic alien incidents to influence pop culture.

TRUTH TODAY

While conspiracy theories and urban legends will never stop feeding the public stories about how aliens really do exist, for one reason or another their existence is yet to be a fact asserted by scientists. However, it is true that direct searches have revealed possibilities of life on other planets. The latest is the discovery in 2012 of a sugar molecule in a distant star system, which is an important building block for RNA and thus, life. However, it is still too early to tell if a complex living system exists anywhere else in the universe.

As children of history, we can only hope that it is a mystery that is resolved in our lifetime. The question is: Do we want to contact aliens, even if they existed? Will it be beneficial for our planet or dangerous? Now that's a mystery for another day!

3

Why Are There No Other Human Species Alive?

'The hallmark of the human species is great adaptability.'

—David Grinspoon

Have you wondered about the intricacies of our planet's biodiversity—how one living genus includes so many different types of creatures? For instance, the Felidae or the cat family includes everything from your regular housecats to leopards, lions and tigers. Same goes for the Canidae or the dog family—that makes dogs, wolves and foxes distant cousins to each other.

These are just two simple examples. The living world is full of such instances. So why is it that there are no other living species of humans alive? Human beings are undoubtedly the smartest and most evolved creatures in this world—so how come none of our species made it? Isn't it mysterious that the only surviving species of the Homo genus now commands and controls the world as we know it? This has had a less than positive impact on the planet as we all know, but that's a debate for another day.

THE HISTORY

Modern humans, or *Homo sapiens*, evolved across the world roughly 350,000 to 300,000 years ago—from other pre-human species. Firstly, we have enough evidence of ancient human-like species such as *Homo habilis* and *Homo erectus*, both evolving more than a million years ago in Africa. Then, we continue to come across news of discovery of bones of extinct human species, newly categorized. For instance, *Homo naledi*—a new species or sub-species that evolved around the same time as modern humans—was discovered in South Africa when hundreds of their bones were found.

However, regardless of the number of such discoveries, it is certain that *Homo sapiens* are the only living human species outliving all of their relatives since around 30,000 years ago—when the last of the Neanderthals died out.

THE REASON

Much earlier, the cause for the survival of modern humans was attributed to their big brains, but that is not true—as other species were also found to have similar-sized brains, proportionate to their bodies.

To know that science still does not have a solid answer to this is astounding, but it's true—we don't know! The most that scientists have been able to do is provide theories on why we have made it so much further than our relatives.

Climate Change

The early hominins (human-like species) mainly ate food from plants while living in forested areas. Once they started moving out into wide open fields with the change in climate, their diets changed to include the meat of animals. This made for a more competitive process in food collection, thus allowing for the slow extinction of weaker species.

> **THE HOBBITS WERE REAL!**
>
> Even if you are not a fan of fantasy literature and movies, you must have heard of hobbits? Yes, the lovable short fictional creatures with big ears! What if we told you that they were real? Well, a human species called *Homo floresiensis* or the Flores man was discovered in an Indonesian island in 2004. Scientists started using the nickname 'hobbit' for them, because they were just 3'3" tall. This caused a legal controversy in 2012 when the creator of the fictional hobbit forbade the use of the name for the human species. That has not stopped the scientific community from using the nickname.

Encroachment

Neanderthals were living in Europe for over 200,000 years when modern humans arrived just 40,000 years ago. Even though the former were used to the cold climate of the region, climate change could have caused them to struggle—which was not an issue for *Homo sapiens*, who quickly adapted.

Hunting Abilities

Homo sapiens were skilled in hunting in both forests and wide-open grounds; they hunted for both small and big prey, and their tools were versatile to help them in their hunts. This was not the same for the other human species, and as such they could not adjust well enough when required.

Art and Language

Even though there are some evidences that other human species made jewellery, it was nothing in comparison to modern humans who started creating a lot of symbolic art, musical instruments and other expressions of creativity. This was important because it became a means of communication among them, leading to language and a more social and complex manner of coexistence. Remember the saying, 'Man is a social animal'? This is probably how it all began.

Genetic Development

Genetic evidence reveals that our genetic make-up changed and parted ways with our relatives at some point. This was when our tools started becoming more sophisticated, our art flourished and we were probably genetically programmed to forge ahead.

ADAPTABILITY: THE BIGGEST TOOL

The most probably hypothesis—as gathered from the previously discussed reasons as well as put forward by some archaeologists recently—is that Homo sapiens could not only adapt to any terrain, condition, weather or situation, but they could hone their skills and tools to master such factors, unlike other hominins. Creativity and social skills furthered this capability.

This was why humans spread to all parts of the world—even places with extreme weather, considered inhospitable—and prosper, while other species started dying out as the planet changed climates, witnessed natural disasters and brought forth newer challenges.

Or maybe we just got lucky. Even though the answer to this mystery probably lies in the 'survival of the fittest' theory, isn't it fascinating, nonetheless, to imagine the hundreds of thousands of years that it took us to come this far?

4

What Is the Taos Hum?

'I'm not completely sure we aren't all living in a hallucination now.'

—Marc Maron

Some individual experiences, if not experienced by others, can be so unsettling that they can raise self-doubt. Are we imagining them? Are the others lying? This is for things we see, feel, and most importantly, hear. Imagine if you were sitting in a room with 49 other people, and you said you heard something that no one else did, would it render your experience null?

Here's a fact. Only 2 per cent of all people hear the Hum, so you may not be wrong.

WHAT IS IT?

The Hum is a mysterious phenomenon that has been reported over time from almost all over the world—but mostly from the UK and the US, for instance the Bristol Hum or the West Seattle Hum. It is a low sound that is reported to be either a humming, a buzzing or a rumbling heard by very few people. Features associated with it are:

- Some people hear it inside buildings more than they do outside
- Some feel it vibrating in their bodies
- Earplugs do not help
- Some can move away from it, but for others it follows where they go
- Both men and women hear it equally—mostly middle-aged people

The Taos Hum is one of the first largest reported cases of the Hum from Taos, New Mexico, in the US. It was first reported in the 1990s.

Interestingly, audio detectors did not pick up anything when investigation was launched. Besides, it was found that different people were reporting different types of the Hum—some heard a low droning, others a whirring, and so on. When tests were conducted, the only unusual activity noted was high electromagnetic field levels. Some reported hearing the sound even after moving away from Taos.

> **MYSTERIOUS, BUT MAGICAL**
>
> Taos, New Mexico, might today be popular for the mystical sound it emits, but it has other claims to fame as well. Famous author Aldous Huxley and actress Julia Roberts have lived in this artsy town.

POSSIBLE EXPLANATIONS

There have been many solid explanations about what could cause the Hum—but they have been different for different instances. Others are mainly theories that seek to describe what caused it.

Machines

This was an obvious one, given that the sound was like a low droning of a mechanical device. It did explain the Hum in many places. For instance, the West Seattle Hum was traced to an industrial vacuum pump.

Spontaneous Otoacoustic Emission

Called SOAE, it is the low sound our ears emit that we cannot hear till we are in a very quiet environment or we concentrate really hard. It is said that 38 to 60 per cent of adults experience them.

Tinnitus

It is a hearing problem that causes people to hear a faint ringing sound due to a disturbance in the nervous and auditory systems.

Psychological Causes

Given that the Hum is heard by such a low percentage of people, another possible explanation forwarded is that it could be just 'in their heads'. Auditory hallucination is thus a possible theory.

Water Bodies and Animals

> **AND IT HUMS ON...**
>
> It is not just Taos where people continue to hear the Hum decades after it was first reported. The Hum in Bristol was reported in the late 1970s, when people blamed it on local factories and traffic. It has been more than 40 years and people there continue to report it.

Ocean waves emit low-frequency tremors, called microseisms, which could be another reason. Besides, some Hums have been traced back to the sound from wasps' nests or animals such as toadfish. However, in case of aquatic animals, it has been debated that it is not possible for the sounds of these fish to travel too far inland to cause any Hum.

CONSPIRACY THEORIES

Moving beyond the reasonable, there is an entire realm of theories that hang purely on conspiracies. One of them is about how the government is conducting secret military experiments, resulting in these sounds. Some others are mysterious submarine communications and even underground UFO bases.

Another interesting one is the High-frequency Active Auroral Research Program or HAARP. It conducts experiments on the ionosphere of the earth and is also rumoured to cause changes in the weather. These experiments are what is said to be causing the Hum.

WHAT HAPPENED IN TAOS?

So why is it that of all the reported cases of the Hum, the one in Taos continues to capture popular imagination? It is because no explanation forwarded could correctly get to the root of the mysterious humming sound that people seemingly continue to hear in this small, laidback community in New Mexico.

It continues to be an odd occurrence that has made its way into the top lists of unexplained mysteries around the world. In fact, it has been incorporated into episodes of crime thriller series such as *The X-Files* and *Criminal Minds* as well.

Do the hearers concerned have super hearing? Or do they all hallucinate? When you are not part of the 2 per cent, it can be easy to believe the latter. For the rest, it is one mystery that needs to be heard to be believed!

5

Is the Bigfoot Real?

*'Bigfoot does not exist because there would be evidence left behind—
hair, faeces, bones, kills, offspring, a carcass—if it did.'*

—Kyle Hill

And yet the massive following and literature it has generated is something you cannot ignore. Only recently, a museum entirely devoted to Bigfoot was inaugurated in Georgia, US. Now that is not the kind of homage you pay to a creature that you think is a myth, right? You don't come across museums dedicated to, say, unicorns, do you?

WHAT IS IT?

In folklore, Bigfoot or Sasquatch is a big and hairy ape-like creature that walks upright, lives hidden in the wilderness, and is usually identified by the gigantic footprints it leaves behind. There have been claims of footprints as long as 2 feet and as wide as 8 inches, some even having claw marks! People who have sighted it claim that it is either black, dark red or dark brown in colour.

SIGHTINGS

According to the book *Bigfoot Casebook*, authors have actually documented over 1,000 sightings of this mysterious creature from the early nineteenth to the late twentieth century. One-third of them have been along the western part of North America, while the others are spread across it. Every region has their own version of Bigfoot—some dangerous, others not so violent. Abundant folklore thrives around this big, reclusive ape, but indigenous tribes—from the Sts'ailes people in Canada to Native Americans in the US—very much believe it to be real.

POSSIBLE EXPLANATIONS

While there have been multiple sightings and claims of evidence of Bigfoot, the majority of the scientific community does not believe in its existence. They have put forth numerous explanations for the sightings—one of them being misidentification. Bears or apes are usually wrongly suspected to be Bigfoot.

Other ways that scientists have tried to rationalize the Bigfoot phenomenon is by drawing similarities to primate species, usually extinct. For instance, species under the genus Gigantopithecus (that died 100,000 years ago) bear similarities with the features we identify Bigfoot with.

> **YOU GOT TO HAVE FAITH!**
>
> Whether you believe in the existence of Bigfoot or not, Americans certainly do. And not just a few of them! A poll in 2014 by a news agency showed that there are more people in the US who believe in Bigfoot than they do in the Big Bang Theory. How you interpret this data depends purely on your own views on the mythical creature!

Another such candidate is the *Paranthropus robustus*, even though it has only ever been found in Africa and not anywhere near where Bigfoot had been usually sighted. There have been suggestions of Bigfoot being a distant relative of extinct human beings such as Neanderthals or *Homo erectus*. Again, none of their remains have ever been discovered in North America.

HOAXES

Bigfoot is probably the first example of popular pseudoscience that took American culture by storm. The credibility of genuine Bigfoot enthusiasts is often lost through the antics of those who partake of hoaxes—just to prove that the creature exists. One of the most famous of these was in 2008, when two such men posted a video on YouTube, claiming they had stumbled upon the dead body of a Bigfoot in a forest. This story got international coverage and the body was delivered in an ice box for inspection, but when it thawed, people realized it was a hoax—with fake hair and rubber feet!

Rick Dyer, one of the perpetrators of the hoax, went on to pull another such stunt in 2014, leading gullible enthusiasts to believe that he was actually in possession of a Bigfoot corpse on which he had DNA testing conducted to reveal that it matched no known animal. He even posted videos and photos of it, but later confessed he had it made from latex and foam.

RECOGNITION BY SCIENCE

Zoobank is an NGO, accepted by zoologists, that assigns species names. It has approved the species name for Bigfoot or Sasquatch as *Homo sapiens* cognatus. This is a big boost in legitimizing claims of Bigfoot enthusiasts that the creature actually exists. The next step in recognizing the creature would be to secure its DNA and get it included by GenBank, a DNA bank whose authority is widely accepted by scientists everywhere.

And yet, there are staunch critics of Bigfoot—and rightly so—who continue to state that there has never been any real and solid evidence of the creature. DNA tests done on its supposed hair samples have always thrown up results to show that they belong to other animals—mostly bears and primates. Besides, another argument against it is that while apes live in the tropical forests of Southeast Asia and central and western Africa—even the mythical Yeti of Nepal—it is difficult for Bigfoot to supposedly survive in a temperate climate in the northern hemisphere.

As of today, investigations and research continue into the existence of Bigfoot. There are university conferences to discuss the creature and actual organizations dedicated to it. It's safe to say that this captivating mystery of the animal kingdom is not dying out anytime soon. Who knows, we might have a definitive answer in our lifetime!

6

Is the Yeti Real?

'There is precious little in civilization to appeal to a Yeti.'

—Edmund Hillary

The Yeti has been a legendary creature that spooked the inhabitants of the Himalayan region and brought Westerners to the East in droves during the twentieth century.

Is it real? How can it not be? People have seen its gigantic footprints; some have even spotted the creature from a distance—majestically walking along on its two hind legs. One of the biggest mysteries in the history of the animal kingdom, the possible existence of the Yeti, has confounded explorers, adventurers and locals for centuries—and it still does.

THE SECRETIVE SNOWMAN

This is a giant hairy monster, living high up in the icy Himalayas, deep in its forests, rarely seen by humans except for the huge footprints it leaves in the cold snow. Believed to inhabit the Himalayan mountains of Bhutan, Tibet, India, Nepal and even Russia, the Yeti—which is also known as the Abominable Snowman or Skunk Ape—is believed to be an ape-like creature that is taller than humans.

It is believed to carry a huge stone as a weapon and makes a distinctive whistling sound. While it will use all fours to navigate the forest areas, it will walk upright in open spaces. According to writer H. Siiger, the Sherpas of Nepal consciously try to avoid sightings of this fantastical creature as they believe it brings bad luck.

The word Yeti comes from the compound of two Tibetan words—*ya* (rocky place) and *che* (or the bear). The name 'Abominable

Snowman' was coined in 1921 by a British soldier. But the belief in the legendary creature goes back even further.

STRANGE SIGHTINGS

The history of sightings of the Yeti go back to the nineteenth century, when trekker B.H. Hodgson, on his trip to north Nepal in 1832, came across a tall creature with long dark hair running on two legs. He believed it to be an orangutan.

In the twentieth century, there were determined attempts by Westerners to scale the Himalayas, in the process of which they came across strange creatures.

For instance, in 1925, Greek photographer N.A. Tombazi saw an upright creature like a human walking in the distance, whose footprints he later measured to be 7 inches by 4 inches. It did not seem to be wearing clothes.

> **'STAMP' OF APPROVAL**
>
> The power of people's belief in a legend can very well be gauged by how Tibet released a stamp in 1966 in honour of the Yeti. Seems a bit much? Well, not when you compare it to Scotland's national animal—the unicorn!

The interest in the Yeti peaked in the 1950s, with mountaineer Eric Shipton taking photos of the reclusive creature's footprints in 1951 during his expedition to Mount Everest. Considered one of the best evidences of the existence of Yeti, these photos have been the subject of many debates and discussions.

Mountaineers continued to sight large footprints as well as bipedal animals in the distance—and among such explorers were Edmund Hillary and Tenzing Norgay. In fact, Norgay claims his father saw the giant ape-like creature twice.

EXTENSIVE EXAMINATIONS

In 1954, there was news of a Yeti scalp housed in a monastery in Nepal. Examined by experts, it was dark brown to black in dim light, and fox red under sunlight. They could not pinpoint any known animal from which it could have come—including the orangutan and the bear.

Five years later, the supposed faeces of the Yeti were collected and examined, whereupon an unknown parasite was found in it.

MYSTERY SOLVED!

In 1983, a Yeti expedition in Nepal's Barun Valley by Himalayan conservationist Daniel C. Taylor and Himalayan natural historian Robert L. Fleming Jr and the investigation following it led to the mysterious Yeti finally being discovered.

But wait, what you see is not always what you get. Remember all the Yeti footprints found over the years? Taylor also came across them in the Barun Valley—the place where even Nepal's king believed the Yeti could be living. Besides footprints, he also came across a number of tree nests and accounts of tree bears by the locals.

> **NATIONAL PARKS THE SIZE OF SWITZERLAND!**
>
> Taylor and Fleming's discovery of the tree bears led to the foundation of the Makalu-Barun National Park over half a million acres in area, and beyond the border is the Chinese Qomolangma National Nature Preserve in Tibet protecting around 6 million acres of natural area. Together, they roughly are the size of Switzerland, conserving wildlife resources.

These tree bears were finally identified as Asiatic black bears. These bears apparently live in the trees for the first two years of their lives to avoid being preyed on by bigger bears on the ground. While doing so, they develop an opposable grip just like humans in their hind paws to help them climb. The hind paws thus develop a thumb-like extension. When walking on all fours in the snow, the hind paw prints are formed over the front paws—not only making them bigger, but also making them look like a hominid or human-like footprint.

So, the Yeti all along was in all possibility the Asiatic black bear, leaving spooky footprints all over the place and scaring visitors and locals alike—or so Taylor is convinced.

THE REASONS BEHIND THE LEGEND

Himalayan wildlife is lush with animals that Westerners are not very well acquainted with. From the Tibetan blue bear to the langur, this ignorance went a long way in keeping the myth alive.

Besides, as one traveller account in the nineteenth century revealed, no one had really ever seen a Yeti for themselves; it was always hearsay.

THE PRESENT SCENARIO

However, it is not easy to let go of the legend that easily. There was news of a female Yeti having been captured in Russia in 2011—later dismissed as a hoax. In fact, DNA testing was carried out in 2013 on all alleged Bigfoot materials—including hair—and the final finding in all of them was that they belonged to bears!

A team of Indian Army soldiers leading an expedition in the Himalayas also claimed having come across the Abominable Snowman's footprints as late as 2019! This, again, could very well be the tree bears' double footprint.

It would be fascinating to discover that the Yeti is an actual creature. But this could be one of those mysteries that live more in our minds than in actuality.

7

Is the Loch Ness Monster Real?

> 'Whatever is the truth, there is no denying that Nessie will continue to intrigue the world for years to come.'
>
> —Jonathan Bright

One of the most lasting mysteries in the animal world has been the legend of the Loch Ness Monster. This slender-necked water creature—resembling a seal or the extinct plesiosaur—has been the object of obsession for people living in or visiting the Scottish Highlands.

In today's time, we are mostly sceptical of such stories and easily brush them off as myths. However, if only one were to hear eyewitness accounts and go through research that peppers the twentieth century, they'd see why the Loch Ness or Lake Ness commands the attention it does.

EYEWITNESS ACCOUNTS

As early as AD 565, there have been accounts of a strange water animal in the region. In 1871, a nearby doctor reported seeing a strange object wriggling and churning in the water, moving slowly at first and then rapidly. In 1933, this creature was witnessed on land! A couple driving by the side of the lake saw it cross the road and go towards the lake—with its 4-foot-long body and 10-foot-long trunk. The next year, a motorcycle rider claimed he nearly hit the creature while riding on a moonlit night.

> **INSURANCE AGAINST NESSIE**
>
> Did you know the participants of a triathlon in 2005 who were to begin the competition with a swim in the Loch Ness were insured for 1 million pounds against possible attacks by Nessie (as the creature is lovingly called)?

PHOTOGRAPHIC AND FILMED EVIDENCES

In 1960, an aeronautical engineer Tim Dinsdale recorded a moving hump-like object in the water. While some believed the object to be animate, others were sceptical. In 2007, another video recording of the lake showed a jet-black object moving fast in the water.

In 1954, sonar readings were taken of the Loch Ness on a fishing boat and something curious was found. Almost 500 feet below the boat, there was a large object that was keeping pace with the boat's movement for over 2,600 feet before contact was lost. Almost 60 years later, another sonar imaging revealed an unidentified object around five feet wide following the boat for a couple of minutes at a depth of 75 feet. Some say that it was probably water plants or algae.

HOAXES AND FAKES

The mystery of the Loch Ness monster has received sceptical backlash because there have been a lot of deliberate hoaxes planted by unscrupulous individuals that have reduced the credibility of other possibly genuine footages or sightings. Interestingly, the most famous photo you can find online of the Loch Ness Monster—called the 'Surgeon's Photograph'—is itself a fake one. The object seen in the photo is a handmade wooden toy devised by three men as a revenge on the newspaper where one of them worked.

> **EXTINCT, BUT ALIVE**
>
> In 1953, a primitive fish called coelacanth was captured alive on the South African coast. This fish was believed to have become extinct 60 million years ago. Similarly, the Loch Ness Monster could very well be a descendant of the plesiosaur, an extinct dinosaur, which got landlocked within Lake Ness.

PROBABLE EXPLANATIONS

According to naysayers, who do not believe that a strange creature of such large proportions could be living underwater for so long in a confined water body offer the likeliest possibilities to explain the monster.

Animals

From birds to eels, elephants to water creatures such as sharks and catfish, there is no dearth of other fauna that can be used to explain the strange sightings. Otters and seals too have been suspected.

Objects and Other Phenomena

Weird-shaped tree parts and logs, ripples, optical effects on water and release of seismic gas are the other ways scientists have tried to rationalize the apparent appearance of the Loch Ness monster.

With so many titillating evidences on one side, but such convincing explanations on the other, the balance continues to keep the mystical creature hanging between legend and reality. Even today, the fascination with Nessie has not abated. There is an ongoing DNA study of the lake to ascertain the strange creatures living in it.

Even if she were real, who is to say she might not have succumbed to old age or climate change and died who knows how long ago. Maybe this will continue to be an unsolved mystery for enthusiasts.

ANCIENT CIVILIZATIONS

8

What Really Happened to the Mayans?

'Those who do not learn from history are doomed to repeat it.'

—George Santayana

Have you heard about the Mayans before? If yes, when did you hear it first? For some, it was when the popular Indiana Jones movie *Indiana Jones and the Kingdom of the Crystal Skull* was released. For others, it was when television and the Internet, years back, carried the news that as per the Mayan prophecy, the world was about to end in 2012. Their famed calendar did not carry past that significant year and, along with a number of other theories, made everyone half-curious and half-worried as the countdown neared.

Of course, the world has not ended. But nor has the mystery behind the collapse of this great civilization. How did such a highly developed society—with such a vast geographical territory and rich culture—suddenly vanish? Let's find out.

WHO WERE THE MAYANS?

The Mayan Civilization was one of the six ancient civilizations credited for ushering in immense developments in all spheres of life. It covered Mexico and the Central American countries of Guatemala, Belize, Honduras and El Salvador. The Mayans were a highly advanced people, dating back to almost 5,000 years. They were one of the first societies to use the concept of zero. Surprisingly, they were also a

> **HISTORY REPEATS ITSELF**
>
> The Mayan Civilization had witnessed a lesser-known but similar collapse earlier in the second century.

civilization that never used the wheel for transportation or pottery. Their agriculture, architecture and tools are proof of their immense skill and craftsmanship. They had built more than 40 cities, filled with intricately designed temples, palaces, sculptures and carvings. However, in the ninth century, something happened that caused the populated Mayan cities to be suddenly abandoned. This continues to be one of the greatest riddles in the world of archaeology till date.

CAUSES OF COLLAPSE

Recent studies have found that the collapse of the Mayan Civilization did not happen gradually, but in waves. There were smaller levels of collapse first, then the major one. This was followed by a slight recovery in certain areas, and then another big collapse.

Dozens of theories have been put forward by historians and archaeologists for their collapse. But there is none that is universally accepted. And even though experts agree on some causes more than others, or a combination of them, it may be a long time till we get to know for sure, if at all.

Overpopulation and Environmental Degradation

One of the more widely accepted theories is that the Mayans probably used up the environmental resources around them to a point that these natural sources could no longer support the growing population. One of the most amazing facts about the Mayan Civilization is that, unlike other civilizations, they did not rely on stable sources of drinking water, but rainwater. A shift in the rain patterns, therefore, could have affected their crops. Besides, the Mayans probably added to this degradation by cutting down their nearby forests for fuel and building structures. Such deforestation and overuse of land could have led to a sorry state of affairs and ultimately to the people slowly abandoning their cities.

Extreme Drought

This is closely connected with the theory of environmental degradation leading to climate change. The deforestation would have led to soil erosion and decline in rainfall, leading to drought. As you know, when drought strikes, there is no cultivation, hence starvation and death would have multiplied across the region. And a long, extreme drought could have caused entire cities to be abandoned. However, critics have pointed out how other regions were hardly affected during the same time. Also, if the drought had caused the people of the classic Mayan Civilization to abandon the cities, they would have moved closer to other sources of water. Despite such criticisms, it is becoming more and more acceptable that a drought did occur in the region, and even if it was not the only cause for the collapse, it did contribute significantly to it.

Constant Warfare

Early researchers of the Mayan Civilization thought of these ancient people as peace-loving people who were governed by astronomer–priests of similar disposition. However, with deeper and further understanding of their culture, it came to be noted that they were a violent people and were involved in many wars. Firstly, they believed in divine right: that is, the king or k'uhul ajaw was a middleman between the gods and the commoners. Secondly, they had complex relations with their neighbouring city-states for military, family (through marriage) and trade alliances. According to experts, when the environmental changes started showing despite the blessings of the divine kings, the subjects must have become disillusioned and the entire traditional system of rulership might have broken down. Further, wars amongst the different city-states might also have led to a breakdown.

Foreign Invasion

Another theory popular among a handful of Mayanists is that invasion by a foreign power led to the downfall and ultimate collapse of the civilization. The attackers are believed to be non-Mayans who arrived in the ninth century, which caused the destruction of the

> **BURNING THE BOOKS**
>
> Only three Mayan books or codices have survived history. The rest were all burnt by the Spanish when they invaded the remaining Mayan cities in the sixteenth century.

people in the next 100 years. As with the other theories, this, too, is highly criticized as there is no explanation for where the people went after the invasion as well as why the civilization was not rebuilt.

Epidemic

Some form of epidemic disease is also believed to have been a factor contributing to the disappearance of the Mayans. The rapid destruction of forest cover for cultivation probably led to a disturbed environment that allowed parasitic insects to thrive. Experts believe that parasites causing severe diarrhoeal illnesses must have struck the population, causing children who survived to grow up to be malnourished and sickly. Other researchers believe that the disease that struck the Mayans was not a human epidemic, but a virus that affected their crops and hence their diet.

> **GIVING YOUR HEART TO GOD**
>
> The Mayans believed that human sacrifice pleased the gods: one ritual involved extracting the heart from the human body!

THE FINAL ANSWER

Although we are not any closer to unravelling the mystery of the Mayan collapse, we can certainly learn from their probable mistakes that scientists offer to us as theories. If climate change or warfare was the reason for such a powerful civilization to be reduced to dust, the current environmental and political scenario provides a scary resemblance to this once great civilization. If we really do not want the supposed Mayan prophecy about the end of the world coming true anytime soon, now is the time to act.

9

The Mystery of Stonehenge

> *'Healing and miracles have been a mystery to men of all times. To some, the phenomenon is frightening, while others find it exhilarating.'*
>
> —Mother Angelica

A vast expanse of land with an odd stone arrangement in a circle. Strange discoveries being made in and around it since centuries. Nobody can say for sure why or how it was built. Welcome to Stonehenge, one of the biggest archaeological mysteries from England, and possibly, the world.

WHAT IS IT?

Stonehenge, located in Wiltshire, England, is one of the oldest megalithic structures on Earth. How old? Historians have revealed that its construction probably started as far back as 3000 BC, which makes it over 5,000 years old. The outer 60 stones are set in a circle, with the inner 15 stones set in a horseshoe shape, making it a total of 75 enormous sarsen (sandstone) stones as large as 4 metres tall and 2 metres wide. Inside the outer circle, there is another circle of 29 blue stones, though there might have been as many as 80 originally. As you might have seen in pictures, the sarsen stones are not just standing, but are also laid on top of each other. The sheer architectural genius of building such a structure at a time when there was no machinery to assist the builders is a huge mystery in itself—as are the identities of the builders as well as the purpose behind creating such a giant monument. No wonder it attracts around a million visitors every year!

WHO BUILT IT?

There is no written record about the reasons behind building Stonehenge.

There are only written records of how Merlin the Magician had aided King Arthur's father in building Stonehenge. The stones were believed to have been brought to Ireland from Africa for their healing properties by giants.

In the seventeenth century, archaeologist John Aubrey claimed that this mysterious structure was created by the Druids or the Celtic high priests. Although this claim has been proven untrue by more recent studies, present-day followers of Druidry still gather at Stonehenge for religious purposes.

However, radiocarbon-dating in the mid-twentieth century revealed that the Celts arrived at the Stonehenge area over 1,000 years after the structure was first erected. The monument as we know it today took 1,500 years to build. Researchers have noted how this historical landmark is a sign of unity among the people of Britain, because it could not have been possible for a small group of people to raise this structure without tremendous manpower and cooperation.

WHY WAS IT BUILT?

One of the first discoveries made about Stonehenge was how the entire structure—along with the heel stone located outside the circle—is perfectly aligned to the winter solstice sunset and the summer solstice sunrise. This meant that it was most probably used as a celestial observatory. However, there were a number of other findings that go on to show that this strange place was probably more than just a hub for ancient astrologers.

> **FOR THE QUEEN!**
> Stonehenge is the property of the English Crown.

For instance, remains of fences and gates older than Stonehenge have led archaeologists to believe that it was probably used as a cattle enclosure much before it became a religious or spiritual place.

One of the most interesting facts that have been revealed is

> **LOOK, DON'T TOUCH**
>
> Visitors used to touch and climb the stones, but now they are not allowed inside the structure anymore.

that this present-day world heritage site most likely served as a sacred healing place. People with different kinds of trauma and deformities from all over the world came here to heal themselves—just like the Sanctuary of Our Lady of Lourdes in France today. This theory is further strengthened by the discovery that the blue stones have a ringing sound—also called lithophones. Such stones are believed to possess mystical healing powers in some ancient cultures. Lastly, excavations at the site have revealed graves that contain evidences of deformities, which means the pilgrims who came here and died were probably buried here.

Even though early researchers claim that it was used as a temple, Stonehenge was probably a place of ancestor worship that also served as a burial ground for people who lived nearby.

HOW WAS IT BUILT?

Once you truly grasp just how heavy the stones used in this magnificent structure are, you can appreciate the immense efforts that would have gone into constructing it. Here are some numbers to help you do that. The average weight of the stones is 25 tons (that's 22,000 kg)! It is roughly equal to six fully grown elephants. And the stones had been brought from quarries and sites over 300 kilometres away. That's more than the distance between Delhi and Jaipur!

Now consider the fact that prehistoric people of the British Isles who built Stonehenge had no concept of the wheel or pulley system. You can now imagine the enormity of the task.

One of the theories put forward by researchers was that the builders transferred the building stones via rafts along the river. Others have theorized that these stones were carried from their original locations by glaciers to their current location.

> **HEAVY RAW MATERIALS**
>
> The heaviest stone in Stonehenge weighs over 40,000 kilograms!

The most popular theory is that a track was created with logs and the stones were rolled along on it. Another idea put forward by researchers is that the stones might have been pushed to the location on a sleigh running on tracks greased with animal fat.

CONCLUSION

Even though a lot of information has been unearthed to solve the mystery of Stonehenge, some facts still remain hidden. Where did the remaining bluestones go? What was the purpose of the deep pits found at the end of the tracks outside the structure? Were the tracks cursed? We don't know. But we do know that this mystifying place should be on your travel bucket list.

10

What Happened to the Lost City of Atlantis?

'I think that we need mythology. We need a bedrock of story and legend in order to live our lives coherently.'

—Alan Moore

Few places in history have attracted the curiosity of people as has Atlantis. Literature, art, cinema and much of pop culture is rife with its mention. Thus, it is very likely that you have come across it somewhere. From the worlds of DC and Marvel comics to the Disney movie *Atlantis: The Lost Empire*, this place has achieved a mythical status in collective imagination.

WHAT IS THE ISLAND OF ATLANTIS?

The first mention of this legendary place was made by the Greek philosopher Plato in 360 BC. He wrote that it existed 9,000 years before him and its stories have endured through poets and priests.

The founders of this island were said to be half-human, half-god. They were a great naval power and a military threat to what he mentioned as ancient Athens. The island itself has been described to be filled with rare and exotic wildlife and rich in gold, silver and other precious metals. However, as Plato's narrative goes, these powerful Atlanteans faced the wrath of gods and nature, as a result of which powerful earthquakes and

> **ORIGINAL USE OF WORD**
>
> Even though Plato is said to be the first to mention Atlantis, the word was used by the Greek logographer Hellanicus 100 years before that.

floods wreaked havoc on their isle, sinking it to the bottom of the ocean. As the saying goes, pride goes before a fall. And the people of Atlantis who were growing stronger and prouder finally met their end.

From the days of Plato till today, the minds of everyone who knows of Atlantis have been fuelled by the imagery of a grand kingdom sunk somewhere in the marine depths, as ocean life continues to swallow it through the centuries. But where is it?

THE LOST LOCATION

It has been said that you can close your eyes and pinpoint to any place on the globe, and there will be at least one hypothesis of how the place is located there. Here are the most popular theories put forward by experts over centuries.

Atlantic Ocean

Given its name, Atlantis is popularly believed to have been situated somewhere in the Atlantic Ocean, especially because that is what Plato's writings on the island say. Islands in Spain and Portugal have been identified as possible locations.

Mediterranean Sea

Connections have also been drawn between Atlantis and the civilization of the Minoans located on the Greek islands of Crete and Thera (present-day Santorini). Said to be the first great civilization in Europe (and being the first Europeans to have used a written language), the Minoans flourished as a powerful people more than 4,000 years ago. However, a huge earthquake that was followed by volcanic eruptions and tsunamis is said to have devastated the society. Ten million tons of rock and ash erupted from the volcano and the people either perished or disappeared entirely, making it another lasting mystery in history.

Antarctica

In the 1950s, American professor and author Charles Hapwood claimed that Atlantis was actually Antarctica, but the shifting of the earth's crust 12,000 years ago pushed the legendary island further up north. Because of the extreme climate in the polar region, the Atlantean Civilization perished and their ancient city became buried under layers of ice.

Bermuda Triangle

Another writer Charles Berlitz claimed in the 1970s how Atlantis was a real continent situated near the Bahamas. However, it was swallowed up by the Bermuda Triangle—another mysterious place dreaded by sailors in the Caribbean Sea.

But that's not all. Scholars have also identified it with America. Others believed that the Mayan ruins were a remnant of Atlantis. It even has an Indian connection—the mythical lost continent of Kumari Kandam!

WHAT WERE THE PEOPLE OF ATLANTIS LIKE?

Plato's works described the ruler and inhabitants as spiritual, upright and highly advanced. However, they later became greedy and evil, which led to their destruction. Some say that Atlanteans were gifted with supernatural and psychic powers.

So, Was Atlantis Real?

Plato's description of Atlantis has been taken literally as well as symbolically by many of his students as well as later writers and scientists. Aristotle believed that Atlantis was a fictional place that his teacher Plato used as a metaphor to teach philosophy. But there were many who believed that Plato was citing real historical facts. This included Ignatius Donnelly, who is known as the 'father of the nineteenth-century Atlantis revival'.

> **PROPHECIES AND PREDICTIONS**
>
> Edgar Cayce, an American psychic, had predicted that Atlantis would rise once again in the 1960s.

He put forward the theory that Atlanteans were a culturally and technologically sophisticated people from whom all ancient civilizations that we know of today descended. The kingdom of Atlantis was where the Biblical Garden of Eden was located and it was the Great Flood mentioned in the Bible that ultimately destroyed this great city.

Today, the mythical sunken island of Atlantis is accepted to be just that—a myth. However, experts agree that incidents in the ancient past—natural and man-made—were inspirations behind the myth-making. One of the most probable events was the sinking of the Greek city-state of Helike in 373 BC during a winter tsunami.

The idea of utopian societies has always fascinated writers and philosophers, so it was no wonder that Atlantis was an inspiration for a lot of them—two of the most famous ones in literature were Thomas More (author of *Utopia*) and Francis Bacon (author of *New Atlantis*).

Has It Been Discovered?

The image of daring ocean explorers finally discovering the lost city of Atlantis has been so deeply ingrained in our minds through cinema and literature that it is something we really want to happen. Back in the days when underwater exploration was not developed, it was easy to believe that there just might be a lost kingdom waiting for us deep down on the ocean bed. However, even the most advanced oceanographers and submariners have not found a shred of evidence of Atlantis.

Enduring Legend

It has been more than 23 centuries since Plato died, and yet the legend of Atlantis persists, having captivated people for generations. It continues to be a popular topic even today—with entire websites dedicated to it. There have been fascinated individuals who have spent—and some lost—their lives trying to unravel the mystery that is the sunken nation of Atlantis.

Why? Because contrary to what Plato wanted to convey of the island as a moral lesson in humility, Atlantis to us is a utopia. A perfect place that is forever lost to us, but for the treasure trove of books, movies and art that keeps its mystery alive.

11

Deciphering the Indus Valley Script

*'While a people preserves its language,
it preserves the marks of liberty.'*

—Jose Rizal

How many languages do you know? The most common answer would be two to four for almost all Indians. When you try to imagine people across the world speaking over 7,000 different languages, it can be pretty mind-boggling. All these languages have a written form—or script. Now imagine this: almost all ancient languages, scripts and writing systems have been deciphered, but that of the oldest and most technologically advanced civilization of the ancient world continues to be a mystery.

Yes, it is the Indus or Harappan script of the Indus Valley Civilization. From the Egyptians to the Mayans, from the Chinese to the Roman, linguists have claimed victory in understanding the languages of all the earliest civilizations, save this ancient Indian one.

What could be the reason behind this? If the people of this time were so developed and promising—with expert town planning and architecture—surely their language would have been advanced as well?

CRYPTIC SYMBOLS

From 3500 BC to around 1900 BC, the collection of symbols used throughout the Indus Civilization is together called the Indus script. Sadly, all the inscriptions found with these symbols are too short to understand whether they are actually part of a language or not.

Appearing alongside animals such as bulls, elephants, rhinos, water buffaloes and even unicorns, these symbols continue to stump experts even today. Do you know a very common animal that does not appear on these inscribed seals and other objects? If you guessed horses, you are right! There are surprisingly no horses found among any of the animals inscribed on artefacts from this era.

IS IT A LANGUAGE AT ALL?

With only 400–700 principle signs in the script, experts have put forward a number of hypotheses as to what the script could actually be. While most archaeologists debate about its language, there are those who believe that the Indus script does not have language signs, but comprises abstract symbols that signify families, clans, gods, religious concepts and the like. Have you ever seen a Native American totem pole? Or a European coat of arms? The significance of the script was compared to such symbolic items.

> **BEYOND THE TIP OF THE ICEBERG**
>
> Since the discovery of the Harappan Civilization in the 1920s, over 1,000 settlements have been identified by archaeologists. However, since it straddles the borders of India and Pakistan where conflict is common, less than 10 per cent of the historical site has been properly excavated. Imagine the secrets we can uncover if all of it were to be dug up!

As mentioned before, with inscriptions too short to be successfully translated and unknown symbols that increase in number with the progress in excavations, it becomes more and more difficult to adjudge the script as one that has an underlying language.

Yet, there are many who do believe it does.

THE TUG OF WAR AMONG LINGUISTS

It is not just archaeological curiosity to get to the bottom of the mystery of what the language underlying the Indus script is, if at all. With different ethnic groups staking their claims, it has a political implication as well—with different groups trying to prove their claim.

The Dravidian Debate

Based on computer analysis and studies by researchers, it has been found that the Indus script might be connected to a Dravidian language. There have been multiple items found in excavations in Tamil Nadu and Kerala on which there are symbols inscribed that bear a fair amount of resemblance to the Harappan symbols.

The Sanskritic Reading

An archaeologist noted its similarity to the oldest alphabet in the world—Phoenician—and claimed that the symbols could be connected to Sanskrit, including many numerals—1 (aeka), 3 (tra) and so on. It has been dismissed for being subjective and unconvincing.

The Indo-Aryan Connection

A popular claim is that this ancient script bears a connection to the Indo-Aryan family of languages, but archaeologists raise doubts about any Aryan speaker—who are known for their travels—to have been around during that time. This is so because there are no horses in the inscriptions—an important animal for a race of people who were always on the move.

The East India Link

As the number of hypotheses increases, they get weaker. This one suggests that the Indus script belongs to the Munda family of languages that are common in East India and Southeast Asia.

The Persian Pattern

Interestingly, this mysterious script is very similar to an ancient Persian writing system called the Linear Elamite. This has caused a section of experts to claim some relation between the two.

THE MANY VEILS THAT GUARD THE SECRET

As already discussed, the hypotheses are many, but the answer is not unanimously accepted or known. What could be the reasons for the failure to unlock this mystery for so many years and decades, if not centuries and millennia? Let's find out.

No Underlying Language

With the Egyptian hieroglyphs, it was reasoned that the language underlying it was Coptic—used among the priests of ancient Egypt. The Mayan glyphs symbolized the language still spoken by the indigenous people of Meso-America. With the Harappan script, no language has yet been unequivocally accepted, which makes it difficult to decipher it.

Short and Not So Simple

The symbols of the Indus script number between 400 and 700 only—with most inscriptions having an average of five symbols, and the longest one not more than 35—that is way too less for linguists and archaeologists to draw any meaning out of.

The Missing Key

Which one would be harder to solve: a huge puzzle with a cheat code or a medium one with absolutely no hints? The latter, obviously! Unlike the ancient Egyptian hieroglyphs that had a Rosetta Stone to act as a key, no such bilingual or trilingual relic has been uncovered that can help in deciphering the Indus script through a language already known.

No Proper Names

When certain proper names are identified—as those for kings or cities—it helps cryptologists unravel codes or symbols in inscriptions when they recur later. However, no such names are known to us, which makes deciphering the script that much harder.

THE MYSTERY THAT LIVES ON

It is not always a tragic thing to have unsolved mysteries on our hands. In fact, it is exciting to

> **MYSTERIOUS PRIZE ANNOUNCEMENT**
>
> If the mystery of the script was not interesting by itself, it became more exciting in 2004. An anonymous donor announced a prize of $10,000 to anyone who could discover any inscription with over 50 Indus script symbols. The longest one yet has only 34, so it is a hard challenge to win!

know that there might be riddles from the annals of history that we just might live to see solved in our lifetime. Ancient DNA testing might reveal the ancestry of the people and thus help us identify the language of their script. Or in due time, with more excavations, we might stumble upon a Rosetta Stone-like key to unlock the secret language of the Harappans. Only time will tell.

12

The Mystery Behind the Statues of Easter Island

'No object is mysterious. The mystery is your eye.'

—Elizabeth Bowen

Imagine coming across a faraway island with hardly any population, and then seeing hundreds of big stone statues that are just weirdly-shaped human heads. What would your first reaction be? Fear? Curiosity? Fascination?

Probably all these and more! Welcome to Easter Island. From aliens to supernatural powers, all kinds of theories have been put forward to explain the 1,000-odd disproportionately large heads, called Easter Island heads, one of the most interesting statue groups of the world.

WHERE ARE THEY LOCATED?

To appreciate the moai—or the statues—in their full glory, you have to first understand the geographical location of Easter Island in the Pacific Ocean. A special territory of Chile, it is one of the most far-flung islands of the world with a very small population. It was declared a World Heritage Site in 1995. There are just around 8,000 people living on the island. The nearest inhabited

> **POPULATION DECAY**
>
> There were only 111 inhabitants on the island in 1877—the lowest ever. Ninety-four per cent of the population either perished or emigrated.

land is more than 2,000 kilometres away! That's more than the distance from Delhi to Northeast India. And in this remote island, far away from the bustling metropolitan cities of the world, in the midst of nowhere, sit a thousand stone heads.

WHO BUILT THE MOAI?

They were created by the aboriginal Polynesian inhabitants of Easter Island, called the Rapa Nui people. It is very difficult to understand the reasons and history behind the creation of these moai, as there is no written or surviving oral history of the island. These early Rapa Nui people are believed to have settled here as early as AD 300, although there are different accounts for establishing the dates. The statues themselves are believed to have been carved between 1100 and 1680.

> **MOAI AROUND THE WORLD**
>
> Ten of the statues have been transported to different parts of the world and are exhibited in museums.

The history of the Rapa Nui people is very interesting too. Already a small population to start with, their entire civilization collapsed and a huge number of them were wiped out. The causes have been pointed out to be environmental degradation or foreign diseases or slave-raiding expeditions, or an unhappy combination of all.

But that's a mystery for another day.

WHAT ARE THE MOAI?

Archaeologists have revealed that the moai are actually sculptures of the ancestors of the Rapa Nui people who they worshipped. It is said that according to ancient Polynesian religions, carved stone objects, when prepared with proper rites, were believed to be endowed with a spiritual power called mana. With coral eyes and majestic top knots (also called pukao), these majestic sculptures were placed on stone platforms (called ahu). According to archaeologists, these moai represent the ancient ancestors of the early Polynesians. Almost all the statues were placed with their backs towards the ocean and facing the island, symbolizing their protection of the next generations of their people on Easter Island.

The only exception to this is the Ahu Akivi—seven moai that

face the ocean. According to legend, Ahu Akivi was built to guide strangers to the island and they represented the seven men who waited for their emperor to arrive.

Interestingly, only about a fourth of the statues were actually installed. Almost half were discovered at the quarry in Rano Raraku, while the remaining ones were found scattered—probably en route to their destination.

Imagine hundreds and hundreds of huge stone statues—averaging a height of 13 feet and a weight of 14 tons—lying in an almost deserted island. Wouldn't it be mysterious to behold? When British explorer Captain James Cook landed on the island in 1774, he would probably have thought so. But what he did also see was that many of the statues were toppled—now believed to have been the outcome of warring tribes. They have now been reinstated.

And one of the most fascinating finds about these statues in 2012 was that even though they are called Easter Island heads, they actually have bodies as well! That's right; beneath the ground they have thighs and knees, with hands over their abdomens. The shifting soils must have covered them up.

> **SIZE MATTERS!**
>
> The tallest moai, Paro, is 9.89 metres tall and weighs a whopping 82 tons!

STATUES THAT WALKED?

One of the biggest mysteries about them, as with any other massive monument in history, such as Stonehenge, is the transportation. Quite a few conspiracy theorists have declared that it could have been the work of aliens! Meanwhile, legends reveal that divine powers were used to make the statues walk to their location—some say that it was King Tuu Ku Ihu who had them transported with the help of god Make Make, while others say it was done by a woman living by herself on the mountain.

Even for the fact-checkers and non-believers, it would seem that the moai were actually made to walk by the workers, by rocking them back and forth while holding them upright, so the statues made walking motions. Not all such statues would have been successfully transported.

Studies have shown that this would be the cause of the fallen moai found on the way from the quarry to their final locations.

MYSTERY FINALLY SOLVED!

Some world mysteries will not be solved in our lifetime—a few of them, probably never. But this is one riddle that thankfully has a happy—or satisfactory—ending. In 2019, a team of researchers cracked the secret as to why the moai were placed in their particular locations.

Given that the Rapa Nui people lived on an island, surrounded by salty ocean water, drinking water would have been a precious resource. And scientists found that the moai were placed at the exact locations where such water sources were found! In a way, these magnificent representations of the islanders' ancestors were actually watching out for them: by guiding them to one of the most important elements for their survival—water.

13

Why Is the Rosetta Stone Key to Understanding Ancient Egypt?

'Less than 1 per cent of ancient Egypt has been discovered and excavated. With population pressures, urbanization and modernization encroaching, we're in a race against time. Why not use the most advanced tools we have to map, quantify and protect our past?'

—Sarah Parcak

Imagine coming across an old locked chest one day that contains the rarest and richest treasures of the world. However, there is no way to open it without a key. And you do not have it. No one does. That is exactly how the whole world felt about ancient Egypt. The mysterious pictures and symbols surviving from the olden times—known as hieroglyphs—were like an open book ready to be read by all, but there was no way to translate or understand it.

And that is why if you love riddles and puzzles, you will truly understand the worth of what is one of the most important archaeological artefacts.

THE MYSTERIOUS EGYPTIAN HIEROGLYPHS

Egyptian hieroglyphic writing first arose around the thirty-second century BC and is said to be god's words or a script created by Thoth, the Egyptian god of writing, magic, wisdom and the moon. As such, this was a script highly favoured by the priests of ancient Egypt, unlike the demotic script which was more for general use. In fact, knowledge of the hieroglyphs was key in distinguishing real Egyptians from foreign conquerors. This script was, in fact, so awe-inspiring that Greek and Roman writers believed it to be a magical language with secret knowledge.

WHY WAS IT UNTRANSLATABLE?

By the fourth century, there were only a few Egyptians who could read this script. The reason was that the hieroglyphic script was favoured mostly by priests and all non-Christian temples were closed down on the order of the Roman emperor Theodosius I around AD 392. There were hardly any documents that explained how this ancient Egyptian script could be read. By the beginning of the medieval period, the knowledge of hieroglyphs became a secret lost in time. There were a few experts who attempted to unravel this mystery in the ninth and tenth centuries, but nothing fruitful came of it.

WHAT IS THE ROSETTA STONE?

Enter the Rosetta Stone—the one missing piece that would be the key that unlocked the treasure chest of ancient knowledge. It is a stone slab that was issued at Memphis, Egypt, in 196 BC. It was inscribed with three versions of a decree that established the divine rule of the new king Ptolemy V after his coronation. To strengthen the Greek kingship in Egypt in 323 BC, he got the stone inscribed with the two important languages—Egyptian (hieroglyphic script on top and demotic below) and Greek.

However, due to the destruction of the Egyptian temples in the fourth century, this stone became lost in the changing architecture of the region—till a soldier under Napoleon Bonaparte came upon it during the French campaign in Egypt in 1799. And after the British landed in Egypt soon after, they took it back to England with them two years later.

Since then, it has been sitting in the British Museum. Despite numerous requests by Egypt in recent times to return this national treasure back to where it belongs, it continues to be part of the British Crown. If this

> **FAME SET IN STONE**
>
> The Rosetta Stone is the most-visited single object in the British Museum till date.

bit sounds eerily similar to the story behind the famous Kohinoor diamond of India, it's probably because it is true. But that's a story for another day.

THE FASCINATING STORY OF DECIPHERING IT

The study of Egyptian hieroglyphs was impossible before the discovery of the Rosetta Stone. Because it contained the same decree in three different scripts, it was the key to understanding Ancient Egypt.

Of the three, the Greek text at the bottom was obviously the first to be translated. Then attempts were made at deciphering the middle text—in Demotic or the 'language of the documents' in ancient Egypt. However, the hardest nut to crack was the hieroglyphic script.

The main credit for unravelling this mystery goes to two people—Thomas Young of England and Jean François Champollion of France. And because everyone wants to believe their countrymen are better than others, there still exist rivalries between the two nations as to whose contribution was bigger than the other!

> **THE EUREKA MOMENT**
>
> Just like Archimedes had his 'Eureka' moment, Champollion too—it is said—had run to his brother's office after making his breakthrough. He shouted 'I've done it!' and promptly fainted—remaining unconscious for five days! Or so his nephew said.

Young made significant observances about the similarities between the hieroglyphic and demotic scripts in 1814, which was a major milestone because both were previously thought to be completely different from each other. In 1821, after correspondence with Young, Champollion was able to work on an alphabet of the characters, which further contributed to the understanding of the script.

ROSETTA STONE TODAY

The study of hieroglyphs was fruitless and impossible before the Rosetta Stone, because it contained the same decree with minor differences in three scripts, making translation work easier. Even though two other older but similar decrees have been discovered since then, the Rosetta Stone has been key to understanding the lost language of the Egyptians.

Now, there is also a digital Rosetta Stone—a complete 3D scan of the ancient artefact that you can zoom into and study it closely.

Interestingly enough, there still does not exist a definitive English translation of the Rosetta Stone, as modern understanding continues to grow about this ancient language. Besides, minor differences between the three original texts have different translators offering different versions.

Viewed from today's perspective, the Rosetta Stone is one of the most treasured pieces of political propaganda from history. While Ptolemy V was merely seeking to re-establish Greek rule by getting this stone crafted—for both Egyptians and Greeks to read and pledge allegiance—he had no idea he was gifting a treasure to the future world. Without it, Ancient Egypt would still be inside that locked treasure chest—with no key to open it.

And you can hardly call it an exaggeration, because if you look up the meaning of Rosetta Stone, it says 'what gives you a clue to understanding something'. So you see, it is more than just a proper noun today!

14

The Mystery Behind the Nazca Lines of Peru

'The true mystery of the world is the visible, not the invisible.'

—Oscar Wilde

The first time you get on an aeroplane, you cannot help but be fascinated at seeing the ground from high up above. The buildings, mountains, trees and everything else start to look so small and different. However, flying 1,500 feet above the Nazca Desert in southern Peru will probably be the most fascinating air experience ever. Why?

The flat ground below is riddled with huge markings that seem impossible to have been made by human beings without supernatural help. All sorts of animals, birds, plants and geometric patterns lie mysteriously on this expansive terrain—silently watching time pass by for centuries.

What are these lines? Who made them? And for what purpose? Some of these questions have been answered by archaeologists over the decades. But some still remain unsolved. Welcome to one of the toughest riddles of South American history—the Nazca Lines of Peru.

WHAT ARE THE NAZCA LINES?

They are geoglyphs or durable motifs made on the ground. They were made on the desert of Peru between 500 BC and AD 500. There are over hundreds of these geoglyphs scattered across the hard desert floor,

> **MISTAKEN IDENTITY**
>
> The Nazca Lines were first mentioned in a book in 1553 by Pedro Cieza de León, a Spanish historian, who mistook them for trail marks.

the widest measuring one kilometre. The combined length of all these patterns comes to a mind-blowing 1,300 kilometres—that is almost the distance between Delhi and Mumbai!

Over 70 of them are patterns of animals and birds such as the hummingbird, dog, llama, lizard, jaguar, fish, spider and monkey. There are images of trees and flowers as well, but most of the geoglyphs are strange geometrical patterns that are as mysterious as they are old. Although these have been around for around two millennia, they were first spotted from the air in 1939.

The Nazca Lines have been declared a World Heritage Site by UNESCO in 1994 and continue to attract millions of tourists to Peru every year.

HOW WERE THESE LINES MADE?

These geoglyphs are generally believed to have been the handiwork of the Nazca culture that thrived in this region. Do you wonder how such lines have survived natural decay for centuries? Ditches were dug by removing the top layer of the ground, which revealed a light-coloured sub-layer with high amounts of lime. This lime hardened and formed a protective layer that resisted the erosion that would have been caused by the winds.

> **CAUSING DAMAGE AT A CAUSE**
>
> The environmental NGO Greenpeace was almost sued by the Peruvian government for causing damage to some of the geoglyphs when their activists visited the area for a campaign.

The windless climate too contributes a lot to the preservation of these lines. The Nazca Desert is one of the driest on earth, with an average temperature of 25 degrees Celsius.

While sandstorms and investigations by researchers are revealing newer figures, some geometric geoglyphs are being eroded due to squatters. Over 100 new geoglyphs have been discovered since 2006, even as the region faces threat of pollution and erosion due to deforestation.

WHAT WAS THEIR TRUE PURPOSE?

Archaeologists, historians, scientists and many others have tried to answer this question, but there is no definite answer yet. Let's look at some of them.

Religious Cosmology

Just like Stonehenge, these lines were created to worship gods as well as for the purpose of being an observatory from where the location of different celestial bodies on significant dates could be observed. Experts have theorized about how the animal figures represent the constellations or counter-constellations—that is, the empty patches of space in between the constellations. The reason they are so big in size is that they can be seen by the deities in the sky, according to some.

Others have noted that it could very well have served the purpose of an astronomical calendar.

Giant Looms

According to an art historian, Henri Stierlin, the lines were created to function as giant looms on which really long threads used to be fabricated. They bear similarity to the textile patterns of the civilization that flourished before the Nazcas—the Paracas. Such fabrics were used to wrap mummies in that period. Stierlin says that the figurative geoglyphs were only made for ritualistic reasons.

Irrigation

Others have pointed out that the geoglyphs were connected to the Nazca culture's water requirements. This Peruvian Civilization was already known for its impressive underground aqueducts. Some have pointed out that the patterns were created to worship deities and invoke their aid in supplying water. Others have revealed how the patterns were tracks connected to irrigation.

Worship of water deities was common in their religion. For instance, the condor geoglyph has been connected to the local legend that when a condor flies over the mountain, it signifies the coming of great rains. The hummingbird figure, too, appears only during summer if there's heavy rainfall.

Other Theories

Many other researchers have put forward many more theories—from the geoglyphs being fertility symbols to venues for events connected with the Nazca's agriculture calendar to even being sacred routes between religious sites. However, these still remain theories, as nothing concrete has been found by anyone that can be offered as proof.

And that's what makes the Nazca Lines one of the most enduring mysteries of history. While they hold the Guinness World Record for being the largest geoglyphs ever, there does not seem to be any conclusive evidence as to why they were made. All we can do is look at them and make our guesses.

15

The Predictions of Nostradamus

> *'Indeed, the hereditary gift of prophecy will go to the grave with me.'*
>
> —Nostradamus

The past is strange. The future even more so. Thus, it is no wonder that if someone's prophecies from half a millennium ago continued to come true even in the twenty-first century, it would be one of the world's greatest mysteries.

Nostradamus—this is a name that you certainly must have come across. Considered one of the most interesting figures in the pages of history, his predictions written over 500 years ago are still considered relevant by people around the world today. Because what he spoke about then are all coming true one by one.

WHO IS NOSTRADAMUS?

Nostradamus, whose real name was Michel de Nostredame, was a French astrologer, physician and prophet who lived in the early sixteenth century. He had a very interesting life and career. It is made further interesting by stories told about him by later authors—so much so that it becomes difficult to separate fact from fiction.

He started out in medicine, using natural remedies to tackle the plague. Over time, he started moving away from the medical to the mystical, dabbling in horoscopes and future-telling. This was when he wrote his first almanac, whose popularity motivated him to write one or more every year thereafter. When he was done, he had written over 6,000 prophecies!

This was also when he began writing his book of prophecies—titled *Les Prophéties*—which contained four-line poems predicting future

HIS PROPHECIES

> **CRUNCHING NUMBERS**
>
> Since his death, there have been over 200 editions of *Les Prophéties*, with more than 2,000 commentaries.

events and was published in 1555. These prophecies were mostly undated and have been translated into many languages.

It is extraordinary that his book of prophecies is still in print today. From the Great Fire of London to the bombing of Hiroshima and Nagasaki, it is astounding how he predicted every great event to come.

For instance, this was one of his predictions:

> *The blood of the just will be lacking in London,*
> *Burnt up in the fire of '66:*
> *The ancient Lady will topple from her high place,*
> *Many of the same sect will be killed.*

True to his words, there was a small fire in a London bakery in 1666, which blazed across the city for three days! Today, we know it as the Great Fire of London.

Another of his prophecies foretold the coming of Adolf Hitler:

> *From the depths of the West of Europe,*
> *A young child will be born of poor people,*
> *He who by his tongue will seduce a great troop;*
> *His fame will increase towards the realm of the East.*

How could someone who lived years, decades, even centuries before, know of things to come? Was he gifted with supernatural powers? Could he actually have foreseen the future, this strange man living in sixteenth century France? A lot of authors and his followers certainly believed so. But he had his share of critics who pointed out the gaping holes in his grand narrative of the future.

HIS CRITICISM

Since his death, there have been many critics of his work who have pointed out that his prophecies were vague, plagiarized and even misinterpreted.

Sources of His Prophecies

When experts started studying his work and searching for its origins in the seventeenth century, they came across a whole lot of other works by past authors from where he had taken inspiration liberally, including the Holy Bible. In fact, some of his references are taken almost word by word from previous works! It was evident to these critics that neither was Nostradamus's work original nor was he gifted with extraordinary powers.

Generalized Predictions

Since most of his prophecies did not mention exact names or dates, his opponents have raised concerns about how they could be used to explain any great event that occurred in the future. The general vagueness of his words has enabled conspiracy theorists to somehow force his predictions into reality on retrospection. For instance, the following could be true of any great flood that has occurred due to climate change:

> *For forty years the rainbow will not be seen.*
> *For forty years it will be seen every day.*
> *The dry earth will grow more parched,*
> *and there will be great floods when it is seen.*

Mistranslations and Misinterpretations

A section of these experts has also noted the poor translations that have somehow changed the meanings of the original prophecies. The English translators did not seem to have much knowledge about sixteenth-century French, hence the original text seems to have been passed down in a sort of Chinese whisper.

Besides, there also have been those that have deliberately altered some texts while translating them so as to make them fit for certain events. This only adds fuel to the raging conspiracy theory fires that

Internet enthusiasts in current times love stirring up.

NOSTRADAMUS TODAY

Despite so much backlash, it is not without reason that the writings of this supposed seer continue to dominate our collective psyche. Maybe he believed that history repeats itself, so things to come have already happened in the past. Maybe he was secretly truly insightful and understood how the future would play out. Maybe he was just faking it. All we can do is wait and watch as history gets made with each day.

CURIOUS ARTEFACTS

16

The Shroud of Turin

'Belief creates the actual fact.'

—William James

One of the most important objects from history for the entire Christian population across the world today is the Shroud of Turin. It is the piece of cloth that Jesus Christ was supposedly buried in, before he was resurrected. Can you imagine anything holier for an entire religious community than the very material that covered the Son of God after he was tortured, crucified and then laid down before he rose again?

No wonder then that this shroud carries with it the faith of a religious community that accounts for nearly one-third of the human population! So, is it the real burial cloth of Jesus Christ then? Or is it fake? Or is it still a mystery? Let's find out.

HISTORY OF THE SHROUD

The Shroud of Turin is named after the Italian city of Turin where it is kept in the Chapel of the Holy Shroud. The metre-long piece of linen depicts the imprints of the face and body of a crucified man—and has for centuries been widely believed and accepted as the shroud or burial cloth of Jesus of Nazareth.

It is said to have appeared in an illustration in a set of twelfth-century medieval manuscripts. However, the first mention of the Shroud is made in 1390 in a memorandum by a bishop to the Pope stating that it was a fake. From Turkey (then Constantinople) to France to Italy, it has supposedly passed through many owners—Byzantine emperors, the Knights Templar, the House of Savoy and finally, the Holy See.

This highly contested fabric from history has even suffered

damages—molten silver burned holes in it when the French chapel it was earlier housed in caught fire in 1532. It has been repaired since then, and almost caught fire again in 1997 in Turin.

Since its discovery till today, it has stood witness to two warring camps—faith and science—over whether it is real, and if it is, how exactly did the imprints of Jesus of Nazareth come about on it?

WELCOME TO SINDOLOGY

The formal study of the Shroud of Turin has been named Sindology—and it is a field that has engaged many historians, scientists and archaeologists over time. Radiocarbon dating of the material reveals that it belongs to the thirteenth or fourteenth century. However, many who believe it to be real have steadfastly refuted this scientific evidence through hypotheses that, in turn, have been proven wrong.

The Shroud, by itself, does not show every detail as clearly as it does in its negative image, which was first observed in 1898. The facial and bodily imprints are clearer, as are other details which researchers have pored over, trying to fathom the actual method of how the image was formed.

Those who believe that the Shroud is authentic are of the opinion that scientific methods are insufficient to understand the creation of the image on it, and that it was a miraculous incident caused during Christ's resurrection. To put it more rationally, John Jackson—a PhD in physics—proposed that some form of radiation that is beyond the understanding of science occurred during Christ's resurrection. Another physicist speculates that it was formed by neutron radiation at the moment of the body's physical resurrection.

These ideas have not stopped researchers from delving deep into Sindology. While some have favoured the authenticity of the Shroud—dating it between 300 BC and AD 400—others have disregarded such findings with opinions, further tests and hypotheses.

Textile Studies

A fabric fragment dated to the first century AD was discovered near the Dead Sea and is said to have the same weaving pattern as the

Shroud, while another from the same time period discovered near Jerusalem has a simpler weave. If you thought that such findings are confusing, this is just the start.

Blood Tests

While some scientists have found the blood on the Shroud to belong to the AB group, there are others who have raised doubts whether the blood was produced at the time of the image, or later, or if it is actual blood at all.

Pollen Evidence

There have been researchers who have pointed to pollen evidences showing that Jesus Christ was buried with flowers that grow only in Jerusalem (his burial place) and only in March–April (which is when he was resurrected). Such studies have been disowned or proven wrong by others.

Forensic Studies

Here again, there are differences in findings by different scientists. Some studies have shown it to be anatomically flawless, showing proof of the stiffening of a body (rigor mortis) that was whipped and wounded. Still others have noted discrepancies in the physical proportions as well as the wounds and blood flows. These researchers have ventured to state that the image on the Shroud was probably painted by a Gothic artist.

> **EXPERIMENTS OF HORROR**
>
> A French doctor Pierre Barbet, as part of his horrific experiment to discover the authenticity of the Shroud, crucified corpses first by their hands and then by their wrists and hung them up to see if they would stay up.

HOW DID THE IMAGE ORIGINATE?

Regardless of whether the scientists uphold or deny claims of the authenticity of the Shroud, they still have the burden of proof to deliver. And this is the biggest question of them all: how did the image come about? As mentioned above, painting was one hypothesis put forward. And there were many more hypotheses that either claim that the Shroud is authentic or that it is fake.

Anti-Authenticity

- Acid treatment
- Old scientific method of photography
- Dust drawing on wood pulp newsprint and transferring it to the linen cloth
- Wrapping cloth around a sculpture

> **THE DA VINCI CONNECTION**
>
> Recent studies claim that the image on the Shroud was faked by Leonardo da Vinci and it was his face that we see on the cloth!

Pro-Authenticity

- Chemical reaction on the fabric from the dead body
- Radiation
- Discharge from the corona
- Result of ointments rubbed on the body before burial

In fact, as recently as 2013, studies still trying to determine the authenticity of the Shroud have taken a 'Minimal Facts Approach' to get to the most likely hypothesis, concluding that it is highly probable that the burial cloth is real.

THE SHROUD TODAY

Even though four French churches and three Italian ones house pieces of burial clothes said to be that of Jesus, they do not compare with the popularity of the Shroud of Turin.

Interestingly, the Catholic Church has not endorsed the shroud as a relic, although it continues to uphold the immense faith that it commands among the people. The scientific arguments and studies about this venerated object continue unabated. However, this has not stilled the faith of the many devout Christians who visit the city of

Turin when the Shroud is put on display.

So, is it real? Or just a forgery by some trickster to hoodwink innocent believers? That's for us to decide. Until then, this will remain a confounding mystery from history.

17

What Are the Dead Sea Scrolls?

'A people without the knowledge of their past history, origin and culture is like a tree without roots.'

—Marcus Garvey

Have you ever had one of those moments when you realized that a song you used to love is actually not the original, and when you finally come across the original one, you are amazed at either how beautiful it is or how perfectly it has been recreated? That is what the Dead Sea Scrolls are to Christians and Hebrews. After centuries of reading copies of their holy books, they ultimately came face-to-face with the oldest-known surviving Old Testament.

As such, they are one of the greatest finds of human civilization in recent times and one of the oldest manuscripts from the annals of history. Their discovery has opened wide the doors of knowledge to the relevance of the Old Testament, the connection between Judaism and Christianity and the understanding of ancient languages such as Aramaic.

THE ACCIDENTAL DISCOVERY

Also called the Qumran Cave Scrolls, they are a set of manuscripts first discovered in the Qumran Caves, a dry region located at West Bank near the Dead Sea near Jerusalem between November 1946 and February 1947. As with most things, the discovery was a purely accidental one. Bedouin shepherds first stumbled upon the hidden caves when they were

> **DID YOU KNOW?**
>
> The longest scroll discovered was the Temple Scroll in Cave 11, believed to have been 28 feet originally!

looking for their lost goats. One of the shepherds threw a rock in the opening on the side of a cliff and was shocked to hear a shattering sound coming from inside. They went in and found handfuls of scrolls stuffed into jars. Not knowing or understanding their value, they sold them in the nearby market and they circulated among different buyers till they came to the attention of researchers.

Interestingly, even after it was found that these valuable scrolls were discovered in naturally forming hidden caves along the Dead Sea, it took the researchers two years to find their exact location and over 12 years to finally find them all! They literally had a treasure trove of hundreds of scrolls waiting for them in not one, but 11 caves.

WHAT ARE THESE SCROLLS ABOUT?

Every once in a while, we stumble upon discoveries that completely change the way we perceive certain things or help us understand them better. These scrolls are just that. They are the second-oldest manuscripts we know of to have survived through the ages. These scrolls contain Biblical and non-Biblical texts that prove that the Old Testament was written before the time of Jesus Christ.

> **TREASURE MAP?**
>
> The Copper Scroll found in Cave 3 reveals that there are 64 underground hiding places throughout Israel that contain treasures such as gold and silver!

The Old Testament is the first part of the Christian Bible that is based on the Tanakh or the Hebrew Bible and contains ancient religious writings believed by both communities to be the Sacred Word of God. The Dead Sea Scrolls is one of the oldest copies of what we know today as the Old Testament, thus proving that the translation of this important holy book is quite precise. In fact, the almost-complete scroll that contained the Book of Isaiah—one of the parts of the Old Testament—is a thousand years older than any other of its known copies.

Written on parchments made of dried animal skin called vellum, papyrus and one even in copper, they are mostly in Hebrew. Aramaic and Greek have also been used to write a fifth of these ancient texts.

The oldest of these 981 manuscripts have been dated to as far back as the third century BC!

These manuscripts were mostly found in fragments, with Cave 4 producing around 15,000 fragments from 500 different texts!

ORIGIN OF THE SCROLLS

Even as these scrolls put to rest a lot of questions about history, they raise a number of them as well. And their origin seems to be the greatest one today. The most popular theory is that they were written by a Jewish sect called the Essenes who hid them in the caves when they were under attack by the Romans in the first century AD.

Others believe that other sects of Jews or even early Christians were responsible for the manuscripts. They are believed to have been housed in the library of the Jewish Temple in Jerusalem, but were hidden in the caves when the city was destroyed by the Romans. Today, almost all of the Dead Sea Scrolls are owned by the government of Israel, but its ownership is contested by both Palestine and Jordan.

PRESERVATION OF THE SCROLLS

For a discovery that was made as late as the mid-twentieth century, researchers had not started out doing a great job of preserving the scrolls. These ancient treasures had lasted a millennium, thanks to the aridity of the region as well as the dry storage containers and long-lasting parchments. However, after their discovery, these delicate manuscripts were stored in damp conditions, taped together with adhesives and generally handled poorly. A number of them were damaged beyond repair before they were moved to a more climate-controlled storage area.

CONTROVERSY ABOUT PUBLISHING

The publication of the scrolls had to wait till 1991, decades since they were first discovered. This was a major source of academic controversy. The scrolls were controlled by a small academic group and neither their text nor photographs were made available to other scholars.

THE SCROLLS TODAY

Anything of value is certain to be forged. From currency to precious stones, nothing escapes the counterfeiter's touch. Since 2002, black markets have been selling alleged fragments of scrolls. No wonder then that some Dead Sea Scroll fragments were recently found to be fake. They were initially bought for millions of dollars by the Museum of the Bible in Washington DC, US!

Meanwhile, researchers have not stopped the hunt for more Dead Sea Scrolls, as new caves continue to be unearthed in Qumran. More than 60 years after the discovery of the 11 caves, the twelfth cave was found in 2017, and it was revealed that whatever scrolls were kept there had already been stolen. Even now, archaeologists are racing against time and such treasure thieves to get their hands first on the rest of the scrolls, if there are any left.

18

The Voynich Manuscript

'When the time comes, I will prove to the world that the black magic of the Middle Ages consisted in discoveries far in advance of twentieth-century science.'

—Wilfrid Voynich

Imagine a botany or medicine textbook hundreds of years old but written in a strange language and filled with even stranger illustrations. So strange, in fact, that no one in this world has been able to understand the book till today. If that sounds pretty simple, you have only just entered the rabbit hole. The deeper you go, the stranger it gets.

Presenting the Voynich Manuscript—one of the most mysterious objects from history. Cryptographers, archaeologists, scientists—there have been no dearth of experts who have dedicated themselves to deciphering what this book is all about, but there still seems to be no absolutely certain answer.

THE ACTUAL BOOK

The Voynich Manuscript is an illustrated book, named after the book dealer who bought it in 1912—Wilfrid Voynich. It is said to have originated in Northern Italy during the Renaissance—sometime between 1404 and 1438. Written in an unknown language, the book seems to be written for medicinal purposes—with most drawings of strange plants and their parts—but its origin and purpose are not known. The alien script it has been written in is now known as Voynichese among researchers.

THE PUZZLING CONTENTS

Since the language in the book cannot be understood, the only way to make sense of it is through the strange illustrations. The manuscript has thus been divided by experts into six parts according to the sketches depicted in every page.

- Almost half of the book belongs to the 'herbal' section—with sketches of unidentifiable plants.
- The second section is 'astronomical'—with circular diagrams of suns, moons and stars. All of them have 30 women holding a star, each arranged in concentric circles. There is supposed to be some sort of zodiacal interpretation behind them.
- The manuscript gets stranger with every passing page. The third 'biological' section depicts women, some of them wearing crowns, bathing in tubs that are connected throughout the section with an elaborate network of pipes.
- The 'cosmological' folio has vague circular diagrams. There are maps of islands with castles and volcanoes connected with each other.
- The 'pharmaceutical' section has illustrations of different plant parts and what seem like old medicinal containers called apothecary jars.
- The final folios are what seem to be 'recipes'.

Given such content, there have been theories about this book being connected to alchemy or a medical treatise on women's health.

THE MYSTERIOUS AUTHOR

The questions this book, without a title or an author, throws up are many—and its authorship is probably one of the most important ones. Although the book was written in the early 1400s, there is no record of it before the 1600s and it was first possessed by Emperor Rudolf II. Since then the book has changed ownership till it finally came to be placed in the Yale Library in 1969. Its

> **A BOOK WORTH KILOS OF GOLD**
>
> Emperor Ruldolf II bought the Voynich Manuscript by paying 2.07 kilograms of gold to an unnamed stranger.

owners have referred to it as 'a certain riddle of the Sphinx' and how 'these obey no one but their master', thus proving that this manuscript has continued to puzzle everyone who has laid their eyes or hands on it.

As to who wrote it, there are a number of hypotheses put forward by experts. Voynich refused to disclose the name of the book's previous owner, which is why many believe him to be the author.

Besides, there is a hypothesis that the manuscript was written as a joke or a challenge to fool and intrigue others. However, cryptographers who have noted the highly regular structure of the words have pointed out that it cannot possibly be a meaningless joke or an unsolvable riddle.

THE SEARCH FOR ANSWERS

In case you thought that no one has been able to put forward any answers about the manuscript, you are wrong. The very first one was put forward in 1921, just nine years after the book came into public notice. One philosopher said that the answer lies in using a magnifier to study the tiny markings that are based on ancient Greek shorthand. This needed to be decrypted to understand the second level of the script and the actual content of the book. This was rejected by other experts.

> **IMPOSSIBLE TO DECIPHER**
>
> Cryptologists who have successfully decoded the toughest ciphers in enemy messages during World Wars I and II have tried to unlock the mystery of the manuscript, but failed.

Since then, there have been plenty more theories, however, none that are universally accepted. Among them, some of the popular ones are:

- It is written in a European language coded in a cipher
- The text is steganographic, which means that the actual coherent content of the manuscript is hidden within the visible text
- It actually contains a natural language—possibly from East

or Central Asia—but is written in an invented or constructed language
- It uses North Germanic dialect
- It is some form of an Aztec language
- A case of glossolalia—or 'speaking in tongues' due to religious fervour or mental stress
- Highly abbreviated medieval Latin
- Vowel-less Ukrainian
- Flemish-based Creole

With so many theories, and none of them absolutely correct, no wonder it is one of the most famous cases that eludes the smartest researchers in the history of cryptography today.

THE MANUSCRIPT TODAY

From Leonardo da Vinci to aliens, there has been no end to wild theories about this book with even wilder diagrams. In the meanwhile, there is some solid science-backed research that is unlocking the mysteries of this manuscript with advances in modern technology.

In 2018, the use of artificial intelligence helped scientist Greg Kondrak realize that the language is actually Hebrew. In fact, according to Kondrak, more than four-fifth of the decrypted words in the manuscript can be found in a Hebrew dictionary. However, since they had no idea about the language, they actually succeeded in translating the first line through Google Translate! It read, 'She made recommendations to the priest, man of the house and me and people.'

However, this is just a baby step and will require concerted efforts from experts in various fields before the manuscript can truly be decoded in its entirety.

19

The San Bernado Mummies

*'Life and death are illusions. We are in
a constant state of transformation.'*

—Alejandro Gonzalez Inarritu

What is the first thought that comes to your mind when you hear the word 'mummies'? Is it an Egyptian pyramid with the mummified remains of people from ancient times? Or is it scary bandaged monsters from pop culture and cartoons? For most of us, mummies definitely mean artificially preserved dead bodies—something that was done thousands of years ago.

But that's not true.

Imagine digging up an old cemetery where you'd expect dead bodies to have decomposed and mixed with soil, but instead discovering that almost all the bodies are perfectly preserved—hair, nails, skin, and even clothes! Meet the natural mummies of the small town of San Bernardo, Colombia—one of the strangest mysteries in recent history.

THE DISCOVERY

This little Colombian town, nestled 5,200 feet above sea level in the Andes Mountains, had always been a quiet, unassuming place. It all changed in 1957, when the local cemetery had to be relocated and a grave digger Eduardo Cifuentes made a startling discovery. As he was digging up the ground of the cemetery where the old remains needed to be moved, he realized that the bodies buried there had not rotted at all! They were all buried in the traditional way—without being embalmed or treated, but somehow, they were preserved.

He began unearthing them and also informed people within and outside the town of this strange phenomenon. Apparently, hundreds of such bodies were found, of which about 14 are today displayed in a mausoleum. The family of these naturally mummified townspeople all got together to exhibit them to a throng of curious locals and even more curious tourists.

THE CAUSE

How does one explain this natural mummification? Well, the people of San Bernardo say that their diets rich in local fruits such as guatita (chayote) coupled with clean water and the absence of chemicals and additives have helped the corpses maintain a pristine, life-like look.

While that explanation could be considered, it still does not explain why the clothes on the bodies had not disintegrated. Experts have theorized that this spontaneous mummification could be the result of the dry weather, coupled with the high altitude of the town and possibly some unique quality of the soil. In fact, it was the natural composition of the soil and some underground gas that naturally mummified the bodies buried in Guanajuato, Mexico, during a cholera outbreak in 1833. However, no such underground chemical cause has been found in the case of San Bernardo.

And even then, that fails to explain why only the bodies of one cemetery in the vicinity should undergo this natural preservation. It is no wonder then that alternate explanations turn to some mystical or paranormal activity.

THE MUMMIES

The mummies put on display at the mausoleum can still be seen wearing the clothes they were buried in. It can be a fascinating—if a little fearful—sight to behold. One of them is dressed in his burial jacket and trousers, complete with his tie. These are not just adult mummies, but there are children as well. Locals

> **HOW TO MUMMIFY!**
>
> Natural mummification usually occurs when bodies are buried in extremely cold or dry places or areas that lack oxygen.

say the bodies look perpetually suspended in animation.

Besides the wrinkling, browning of the skin in some and paleness in others, there's absolutely no sign of rotting. This is even more surprising, given the fact that the exhibit does not boast any pressure or humidity control. The doors stay open during the day, allowing in people and the natural air to drift in and out.

Being discovered just over 60 years ago, these mummies are a part of our modern history. The living identities and photos of the mummies have been hung next to their remains—reminding us that they are not centuries-old unknown strangers, but real people who have lived in this town and now rest here in their after-death body.

And this is why the mystery of their mummification is even more tangible. There has been no explanation about this phenomenon that checks all the puzzling boxes. And a mystery it shall probably remain.

20

The Antikythera Mechanism

*'One rule of invention: before you
can invent it, you have to imagine it.'*

—James Gunn

Some discoveries from history are so wondrous that it is difficult to believe that there was nothing supernatural involved in them. One such discovery is the Antikythera Mechanism, an ancient invention that was so far ahead of its time, it is called the world's first computer!

THE OBJECT

This is an ancient analogue computer that was invented by Greek scientists to predict astronomical positions of the sun, moon and planets as well as the occurrence of eclipses. This helped them prepare their calendars as well as plan astrological events well in advance. But that is not all; it also helped the ancient Greeks keep track of the four-year cycle of the Olympic Games.

The device itself was composed of 82 separate fragments and included 30 bronze gears and could be operated by a hand crank—an engineering feat that was unimaginable for a civilization in the second century BC. Yes, that is how old it is believed to be!

Researchers believe that it was once placed inside an upright rectangular box that had dials and inscriptions on the front as well as in the back. About the size of a shoebox, this case had Greek zodiac signs and calendar dates in the front. By moving the dial to any one of the 365 days marked on the face, one could tell the exact position of the sun and the moon.

THE DISCOVERY

It was probably a stormy night when an unfortunate ship laden with all sorts of cargo including the mechanism crashed near the Greek island of Antikythera (from where it gets its name). The ship, with all its goods, sunk to the bottom and it lay there for a good 2,000 years before it was finally discovered by a team of explorers in 1901.

> **GOOGLE DOODLED IT**
>
> Google marked the hundred-and-fifteenth anniversary of the discovery of the Antikythera Mechanism by designing a Doodle on 17 May 2017.

All the items retrieved seemed far more interesting to the researchers than an unassuming wood and metal lump that lay unnoticed for almost two years. This was the mechanism whose value was not realized next to the fascinating bronze and marble statues, pottery, unique glassware, jewellery and coins salvaged from the wreck. It was in 1902, when an archaeologist discovered a gear wheel in the decomposing lump, that attention turned towards it.

THE INVESTIGATION

At first it was believed to be some sort of an astronomical clock. It took another half a century for technology to develop enough to be able to study the Antikythera Mechanism properly. Modern computer X-ray and surface scanning were finally able to help scientists study the disintegrated device and the inscriptions on it more closely.

A number of teams have put forward reconstructed models of what the original mechanism might have looked like. However, none of them are universally accepted. But some scientists are of the opinion that the mechanism, being handmade and thus prone to human errors of execution rather than planning, was probably not completely accurate in displaying the exact calculated astronomical positions.

That said, this complex clockwork mechanism is a symbol of the immense advancement of the ancient Greeks—and its origin still constitutes one of the biggest mysteries. It is today housed safely at the

National Archaeological Museum in Athens in three separate pieces, along with artistic replicas of how the original is believed to have been. The remains of this magnificent invention are now too delicate to handle and have rusted away to almost a shell of what they probably were, 2,000 years ago.

ITS ORIGIN

A mechanical sky chart of such detail being imagined, planned and designed at least 1,000 years before such devices actually started being used in medieval Europe is a fact that still astonishes many. So much so, that conspiracy theorists have hinted at the possibility of aliens assisting in its construction!

While it may be an interesting theory to pursue, most archaeologists now believe the ship to have originated in the Greek island of Rhodes, where the second-century philosopher Posidonius ran a school of astronomy. It is believed that the mechanism was used to teach planetary movements. In fact, writings of the first-century Greek philosopher Cicero speak of a similar device being designed by Posidonius himself—though historians are not sure that it was the same as the Antikythera Mechanism. Instead, an astronomer named Hipparchus of Rhodes is actually believed to have been consulted in the building of this computer.

> **SOLAR SYSTEM OF FIVE PLANETS!**
>
> The mechanism was designed to tell the planetary positions of Mercury, Venus, Mars, Jupiter and Saturn—the only five planets known to the ancient Greeks.

In fact, Greek mathematician and astronomer Archimedes is also said to have designed an instrument to predict the movement of the sun, the moon and the five planets known at the time. This goes to show that the ancient Greeks had enough knowledge to imagine and invent complex astronomical calculators as these during their times. This knowledge could have spread to the rest of Europe, after which later devices were crafted.

But why did such mechanisms—used in making mechanical

astronomical clocks—only become popular since the fourteenth century in Europe and not before? There have been discoveries of other mechanisms like the geared calendar attached to sundials from the fifth- or sixth-century Byzantine Empire, but such examples are few and far between—almost as if the knowledge got lost somewhere in between.

That is another mystery that haunts this ghostly mechanism from millennia ago—one that historians can only take guesses at, but have not been able to really solve.

21

The Aluminium Wedge of Aiud

*'If you haven't found something strange
during the day, it hasn't been much of a day.'*

—John Archibald Wheeler

On that note, I am presenting to you a curious artefact from the annals of history—known as the Aluminium Wedge of Aiud. It is, as its name says, a wedge of aluminium—roughly 2 kilograms in weight—that was discovered in Aiud, a city in Transylvania, Romania. Yes, that name already sets the tone for a spooky—as well as interesting—story!

OUT-OF-PLACE ARTEFACTS

Now, what this mysterious object is called is an out-of-place artefact, or OOPA for short. It refers to any object with features that seem too advanced for the time it belonged to. Archaeology and history are littered with several such OOPAs. These objects have been used by some to bolster claims that modern science overlooks these undeniable evidences, proving the existence of chronological anomalies. Either that, or else such advanced technologies in such early times could be explained by only one phenomenon—extraterrestrial life!

There is a reason why scientists are critical of any object that is claimed to be an OOPA—because more often than not, it is either a hoax, or dated wrongly, has a different origin, or has a more logical explanation.

DISCOVERY OF THE WEDGE

Coming to the Wedge of Aiud, it was discovered in 1974, along with bones of an ancient elephant called mastodon, under 35 feet of sand during a construction project. It lay in the Museum of History of Transylvania for two uneventful decades, gathering dust—until editors of a UFO magazine chanced upon it in the 1990s. And the rest, as they say, is history.

Well, what we mean is that it immediately sparked widespread interest for being an OOPA. The mastodon bones discovered alongside it were seen as evidence that the wedge too was at least 11,000 years old! This is made interesting by the fact that aluminium was not extracted or used before 1825.

Conspiracy theorists have even suggested that it is a piece of a UFO—or something a time traveller probably left behind. There are still forums on the Internet avidly discussing this mysterious object that suddenly appeared in history, much before it possibly should have.

> **INDIA'S FAMOUS OOPA!**
>
> The famed Iron Pillar in Delhi is one of the many OOPAs believers swear by. An astonishing structure built before AD 1000, it has not rusted—even though it has been facing the elements of nature for over a millennium. This points to the metallurgical skills of the ancient Indians, which were certainly advanced for the time. However, in recent times, the pillar has seen some oxidization at its base, which critics have used to refute claims of OOPA enthusiasts.

CRITICISM

However, even the greatest of mysteries can sometimes be solved—and can turn out to be disappointing. After metallurgical tests (the technique or science of working on or heating metals) were conducted, the results showed that the metal of the wedge was similar to the alloy called duralumin, known to rust quickly, which explains its oxidized layer. However, it is believed that the layer was formed over 400 years ago, which is still long before aluminium was discovered. Secondly, critics have also pointed out how the wedge is suspiciously similar to the teeth of excavators.

These naysayers opine that the wedge or excavator tooth probably came loose at a previous dig at the area, during which the mastodon bones were probably missed. Rationally, that is the only logical answer to this strange piece of metal. Because if this did not happen, then its history is certainly mired in some inexplicable mystery.

22

The Bog Bodies of Northern Europe

'Life itself is but the shadow of death, and souls departed but the shadows of the living.'

—Thomas Browne

Have you wondered what happens when we die? Religion has a lot to say about this. From reincarnation to becoming one with the universe, many explanations are offered for the soul. But what about our body? Again, according to religion, some are cremated, others buried, and so on. Ultimately, it is our body—with its skin, flesh, bones and organs—that becomes one with nature.

And yet, what if I told you that there is something in nature itself that can preserve our bodies for not hundreds, but thousands of years? This shocking discovery has been made in many places of Northern Europe, where hundreds of perfectly preserved bodies have been discovered since the seventeenth century.

How have these bodies survived the ravages of time? And why are they only found in Northern Europe? Let's dive into this mystery of nature.

THE BOGS

In ancient Egypt and a number of other cultures, people used to deliberately preserve the bodies of the dead through the process of mummification. However, the naturally preserved bodies that we are speaking of are very different. These bodies are mummified in peat bogs. Peat is a naturally occurring fuel that is formed from decomposed vegetable matter in certain swampy areas.

Only certain unique conditions allow for the preservation of dead bodies in these bogs—highly acidic water, low temperatures and lack of oxygen. The swamps of Northern Europe meet all these criteria—and thus have contributed to the formation of most of the bog people.

> **THE AMERICAN BOG PEOPLE**
>
> Not just Northern Europe, the US too boasts of its own bog bodies. However, unlike the bogs found in Europe, the bogs in the US are wetter—so they preserve the skeletons, but not the skin or organs, although 100 skulls with brains have been discovered. The bodies in the US are 5,000 to 8,000 years old.

Just the way vinegar pickles fruits and vegetables and preserves them, so do bog acids preserve mammalian tissues. The lack of oxygen prohibits growth of organisms, thus negating decomposition. These conditions allow the body as well as internal organs to be well-preserved, while tanning the skin severely. Also, the high acid content leaches calcium from the bones—which either dissolves them or makes them rubbery.

Bodies that were placed in these bogs between winter and early spring, when the temperatures were the lowest, were best preserved.

THE BODIES

If you met the Tollund Man, you wouldn't believe that this perfectly preserved body has been around since the fourth century BC! From his light stubble and eyelashes to his leather cap, he seems to have been suspended in space and time as the world sped onwards hundreds and thousands of years.

Discovered in the village of Tollund in Denmark in 1950, he is one of the best-studied specimens of this extraordinary natural phenomenon. There are over a hundred such specimens all over the continent.

The bodies found in these areas have been dated from over 10,000 years ago! The latest ones found date back to World War II. While a lot of them are found to be in different states of preservation, there are quite a few that are exceptionally well-preserved—like the Tollund Man.

The maximum number of bog people that have been discovered

belonged to the Iron Age—discovered in bogs across Denmark, Ireland, Germany, the Netherlands and the UK. Nails, hair, clothes, headgear, as well as the contents of their stomachs, are found to be preserved. But how did they end up in these swamps in the first place? Who put them there? And why?

THE BURIALS

Punishments

Their first discovery in modern times dates back to 1640 in Germany. Before that, Roman historian Cornelius Tacitus in the first century AD had opined that Germans used to punish criminals by killing them and burying their bodies in the bogs. Later experts were sceptical of this. It did turn out to be true for the most part—there were bodies discovered to have had suffered violent deaths, with grave injury marks, cuts, stabs and strangulations—even beheadings!

The Tollund Man himself was discovered with a rope around his neck. Another one, the Old Croghan Man, has been found with deep cuts under his nipples. There are many other such instances from the swampy corridors of the bog people's history.

Offerings to the Gods

Archaeologists have also theorized that a number of bodies were buried in the bogs and pinned down by sticks and stones, as sacrificial offerings to the fertility gods. They were found with objects such as bronze, sometimes gold, necklaces, anklets and bracelets—as votive offerings for the spirits beyond.

Either way, the bogs were a burial ground of sorts during the Iron Age and later—where victims of gruesome torture and punishment as well as human sacrifices were lain, only to be discovered in their near-perfect conditions thousands of years later.

THE BLESSINGS OF MODERN SCIENCE

There was a time, back in the seventeenth and eighteenth centuries, when people did not understand the historical significance of the bog bodies. They used to cremate or bury them as and when they found them, while digging up the peat from the bogs to use as fuel. It was the Crown Prince Frederick of Denmark in the 1940s who was key in rousing national as well as global interest in the bog bodies as possibly being remains of a much earlier period.

He ordered that one such body—which was found to have been buried with glass beads and a bronze pin—be sent to the National Museum for examination.

> ### THE OLDEST BOG BODY IN THE WORLD
>
> The Koelbjerg Man is the oldest—dating back to 8000 BC—and was discovered in Denmark. First thought to be a woman, he is believed to have been over 6 feet tall and 20–25 years of age. He belonged to a culture in the Early Mesolithic Period in Denmark called the Maglemosian culture. People of this culture used to live in wetland environments, which explains the Koelbjerg Man's remains in the peat bogs.

Since then, science and technology have come a long way. As modern archaeological methods improved, these bodies were dug up and handled with more care since the twentieth century. Today, subsurface radar allows scanning of peat bogs to locate bodies underneath. Radiocarbon dating also allows one to tell the bodies' exact time of death. Forensic facial reconstruction today tells us how the bog people might have looked like when alive.

Modern science might have explained how the bog people continued to occupy their skin up to 10,000 years beyond their death, but it will never take away the sense of wonder you feel the first time you look at a specimen up close. That's when you realize that mysteries can be solved and yet be mystifying.

DEATHS AND DISAPPEARANCES

23

Did Netaji Subhas Chandra Bose Really Die in a Plane Crash?

'Do you not know that a man is not dead while his name is still spoken?'

—Terry Pratchett

When it comes to naming the heroes of the struggle for Indian independence, Netaji Subhas Chandra Bose is one of the first freedom fighters that comes to our mind. From being the Youth Congress president to All India Congress president, his rise in pre-independent Indian politics was meteoric. His brand of defiant patriotism led him to organize many civil disobedience movements and mass protests, getting him arrested 11 times! The Indian National Army (INA) that he organized fought the enemy in many places in Burma (present-day Myanmar). However, the fate of this army was doomed once Japan surrendered at the end of the war.

Your schoolbooks will tell you that this unforgettable hero died on 18 August 1945 after his plane crashed in Taipei (Taiwan). But did he? There are several reasons why many Indians then, and even now, never believed this news. Why?

- There have been no photographs of him once he was admitted to a hospital in Japan after the plane crash or of his body after death.
- The only evidence we have of his death are the verbal accounts of the doctors and his companion on the flight.
- No one else saw the body.
- No death certificate was immediately issued.
- And lastly, when Bose's remains were examined 60 years after

his death, it was found that the ashes weren't his at all!
- There have been documents as well as first-person accounts of people who have met him after 1945.

THE 'OFFICIAL' STORY

The widely accepted story is that on 17 August 1945, he and his secretary Habib ur Rahman boarded a Japanese plane to go to erstwhile Manchuria. And that's when the tragedy happened.

On 18 August, when the flight was taking off after a stop at Vietnam between 2 p.m. and 2.30 p.m., there was a loud bang. Out fell part of the engine and the propeller! The plane crashed, broke into two, and exploded in flames. Bose and Rahman tried to escape, but the exit was blocked with luggage. The only way out was through the broken front, but it was on fire. And Bose was drenched in gasoline. This did not stop him from attempting to escape. He did make it out with his secretary, but he caught fire and came out like a human torch!

He was quickly taken to the hospital and treated for his severe burns. The doctors were shocked at how he could still speak so clearly after such an ordeal. However, this situation did not last long and he was declared dead between 9 p.m. and 10 p.m. His body was cremated on 20 August and the Japanese media announced his death on 23 August.

THE 'REAL' FACTS

People tend to believe what the authorities tell them. When the senior members of the INA back in India received the news of Bose's tragic death and refused to believe it, it was natural that the common people were unsure too. Even Mahatma Gandhi himself had initially claimed Bose's death to be fake.

A number of conspiracy theories arose after the news of his death. Most of them revolved around how he was either in Manchuria, which was occupied by the Soviet army, or that he had been taken prisoner by them, or how the army had helped him go into hiding at a secure location.

In 1946, Lakshmi Swaminathan, a member of the INA, declared that he was in China. Historians Christopher Bayly and Tim Harper talk of powerful rumours about Bose preparing to return to India and march to Delhi. What started happening soon is curious. They say that seeing is believing. And Bose—dead in the news, but very much alive to the people—began to be seen everywhere!

As the years went by, people kept waiting for Bose to make his public appearance. And when that did not happen, and years turned into decades, the mystery kept growing.

> **POST-DEATH SIGHTINGS**
>
> According to historian Gordon S. Wood, one person claimed that he had 'met Bose in a third-class compartment of the Bombay Express on a Thursday', after his apparent death!

QUESTS FOR TRUTH

There were several investigations into the incident, each attempting to stop the rumours that Bose's death in a plane crash was false and misleading. The reports of the first three commissions verified that Bose died from burn injuries after the crash, as did the Japanese government's report of 1956.

Thirty years later, a final attempt was made to put all theories to rest by setting up the Mukherjee Commission in 1999 under retired Supreme Court judge Manoj Kumar Mukherjee. The report stated that Rahman and the Japanese authorities had planned Bose's safe passage to the former USSR secretly!

> **REVELATIONS FROM ABROAD**
>
> It was testified before the Khosla Commission by former Congress MP S.N. Sinha, that a Russian interior ministry agent named Kozlov had told him of Bose's imprisonment in Siberia. This was supported by a German intelligence agent, Karl Leonhard. This evidence was ignored by the Commission.

It also revealed that the ashes of Bose resting in the Renkoji Temple in Tokyo actually belonged to Ichiro Okura, a Japanese soldier who died of a heart attack. Even the Taiwanese government stated that there were no plane crashes in Taipei between 14 August and

20 September 1945. The Indian government refused to accept the findings of this report when it was finally submitted in 2005.

Researcher Dr Purobi Roy discovered that Bose had arrived in Russia from Taipei before the end of World War II and was secretly kept in the Russian prison camp in Siberia in 1945-1949 by Josef Stalin. She even produced his photo taken in the prison there.

The Indian ambassador to Moscow, Dr Sarvepalli Radhakrishnan, was also said to have had a secret meeting with Bose on his visit to the USSR. On his return, Radhakrishnan had informed the newly appointed first Indian Prime Minister Jawaharlal Nehru about it.

The Indian government, however, was not very helpful in taking action despite the strong evidence presented time and again.

THE ROOT OF THE MYSTERY

Supporters of the claim that Bose did not die in the plane crash firmly believe that the Indian government had full power to extract the INA leader from the USSR but they didn't try. They put the blame on the ambitious nature of Jawaharlal Nehru and his attempt to maintain his powerful position of prime minister by deliberately withholding important evidence of Bose's survival. There have been accusations against the government of newly independent India of having destroyed crucial documents pertaining to Bose.

In fact, the Nehru government even spied on Bose's family for 20 years after his disappearance. The question that everyone raised was: Why? Did the government know that Bose was still alive and was nervous about his return to India? If he did, how would that affect those in power? Would they be threatened if Bose formed a powerful opposition, just like he had united millions of Indians to take up arms against the British in the early 1940s?

LINGERING LEGENDS

There were many more myths about this great Bengali freedom fighter than just his imprisonment in Siberia. Bose was always a master of disguise, escaping India and travelling to the USSR by crossing the Afghanistan border after expertly covering up his identity. So it was expected of him to continue doing this after 1945 as well. Some old associates of Bose formed the Subhasbadi Janata in the 1950s—an organization that promoted the story of how the leader returned to India and turned into a sadhu.

The Sadhu of Shoulmari

As per legend, he became the chief sadhu in an ashram in Shoulmari, North Bengal. This myth was perpetuated far and wide, thanks to the Janata's published material that included newspapers and magazines.

This narrative was a broad one. Some of the interesting anecdotes it offers are:

- Bose had walked across India several times
- He secretly attended Mahatma Gandhi's cremation in 1948
- He first became a yogi at Bareilly in a Shiva temple
- He practised herbal medicine and provided cures for different illnesses
- He finally set up an ashram at Shoulmari and then retreated there as the head sadhu

Despite the actual chief sadhu denying that he was Bose and several of Bose's close aides seconding that after meeting the sadhu, the story still spread. The sadhu finally died in 1977, after continuously opposing the rumours till his death.

Bose as Bhagwanji

Another enduring myth about Bose's post-war life was that he turned into a hermit on his return to India and lived as one Gumnami Baba or Bhagwanji in Oudh, Faizabad, Uttar Pradesh. It is still a raging hot topic in the state, especially as his niece claimed that the Baba was none other than Bose. This theory becomes more believable when you learn that after Bhagwanji's death, his belongings were found to contain notes and letters that strongly suggested his hidden identity as Subhas Chandra Bose. When his followers were questioned about it, they confessed that Gumnami Baba was Bose in disguise, but they could not reveal the fact earlier to protect his identity.

Till today, nothing has been proven.

SO, HOW DID HE REALLY DIE?

If the plane crash was a lie and Subhas Chandra Bose did not really die in Taipei, how did he meet his end and where?

There have been as many convincing theories about it as there have been wild speculations. The most accepted one is that he probably died or was killed by the Soviet regime in 1956.

Others, such as Major General G.D. Bakshi, believe he was tortured to death by the British in prison. Bakshi states this in his book, *Bose: The Indian Samurai—Netaji and the INA Military Assessment*.

Those who support the theory of Bose as the hermit Bhagwanji believe he lived till 1985.

NETAJI'S LEGACY TODAY

A legend in life, a myth after death—Subhas Chandra Bose keeps on living through these mysterious stories that will continue to be passed down from generation to generation. Even today, the West Bengal government and his own family continue to demand that his ashes be returned to India and all secret government files about him made public.

What would happen if the ashes were brought back and it was again found that they really do not belong to Bose? Would it mean that people have been fed lies for all these decades? Or would it open the way for yet another investigation—the ultimate one where the actual truth would finally be revealed?

And if tests reveal that the ashes are truly Bose's, it would finally close the chapter to the most mysterious death in the history of the world.

24

Where Is the Final Resting Place of Razia Sultana?

'Well-behaved women seldom make history.'

—Laurel Thatcher Ulrich

The number of men in great positions throughout time has been aplenty, but there have been equally powerful women too who have etched their names in history throughout the world. And in India, when you look for such names—before Indira Gandhi or the Rani of Jhansi or even Devi Ahilyabai Holkar—there is one that shines bright. She is Razia Sultana, the only female ruler of the Delhi Sultanate. Her death is as controversial as her life was—and the mystery surrounding her grave has added a deeper hue to her colourful legacy.

WHO IS RAZIA SULTANA?

When one comes to know that she was an emperor of Delhi, it is automatically taken for granted that she belonged to a royal family. Far from it actually. She was actually the daughter of a Turk slave, Shamsuddin Iltutmish. He was bought by and became a favourite of the first Sultan of Delhi, Qutbuddin Aibak. Aibak gave his only daughter Turkan Khatun or Qutb Begum in marriage to Iltutmish. From this wedlock was born Razia Sultana.

When Qutbuddin died, he was succeeded by Iltutmish. While Iltutmish ran the affairs of

> **SECULAR AND BENEVOLENT QUEEN**
>
> Razia Sultana is said to have mingled among her people other regular rulers and fiercely protected the culture and interests of her Hindu subjects.

the court, little Razia would be allowed to be present around him. In time, she was trained to run the kingdom—in case the need ever arose. This was a privilege enjoyed by quite a few princesses at that time, despite beliefs to the contrary. With time, she exceeded expectations of others and far surpassed them—giving Iltutmish the confidence to name her his heir apparent.

With the king's death and the assassination of her mother and her half-brother Ruknuddin Firuz who rose to the throne for only six months, Delhi saw, for the first and only time, an empress sit on the mighty throne in 1236. While the nobility had its reservations and reluctance to be ruled by a woman, Razia displayed every quality required of a ruler.

LOVE, LIES AND WARS

To change the famous Spiderman quote, 'With great powers come great controversies.' On the one hand, Razia Sultana was said to be in love with her childhood sweetheart Malik Ikhtiaruddin Altunia, the governor of Bhatinda. On the other, there are tales of a forbidden love between her and an African slave, Jamaluddin Yakut. While some historians say that Yakut was just a close friend and advisor to the queen, others such as Ibn Battuta have commented on the intimate nature of their relationship. Reminiscent of the rise of Iltutmish in Qutbuddin Aibak's court, Yakut too rose in Razia's court—to the position of the commander of commanders, much to the contempt of the nobility.

She was already resented for being a female ruler. Liaising with a slave-turned-nobleman became the final straw that broke the camel's back. So, when the news of this supposed illicit affair reached the ears of Altunia in Bhatinda, he led a rebellion against the queen and Yakut. Yakut was killed and Razia Sultana was captured. To keep her father's dream of her ruling India alive, Razia did marry Altunia. Meanwhile, her brother Muizuddin usurped the throne in Delhi. And when Razia, along with her now-husband Altunia, led a siege to recapture her kingdom, she was defeated and had to flee.

And that is where the mystery begins.

HOW DID SHE DIE?

There seem to be multiple accounts of her death, and as a result, a number of claims as to where she is actually buried.

- Legend has it that the queen died on the battlefield from an arrow shot to her heart as she was crying over her dead husband's body.
- The most accepted story is that when the troops accompanying the couple abandoned them, Razia and Altunia were killed by the enemy just outside Delhi in 1240.
- Another account is that they fled to Bhatinda and attempted another advance against Delhi, but were defeated. They were later assassinated by zamindars in Kaithal.
- In another version of the story, she apparently escaped on her horse in a man's disguise and was sheltered by the Kaithal Jats. However, when a fight broke out among them, they killed her.
- Another historian says that she was killed by bandits in a forest when she was returning from the battle on an elephant. However, since Razia Sultana rode her horse to battle, this account is not accepted.
- There are even accounts of her being murdered by Altunia after the war!

WHERE IS SHE BURIED?

Needless to say, the jury is still out on the death of Queen Razia. No wonder then that we have not one, not two, but three possible graves where she may have been laid.

> **MONEY DOWN THE...GRAVE!**
>
> While the Archaeological Survey of India (ASI) has recognized Bulbulikhana as Razia Sultana's tomb, the government of Haryana has spent ₹58 lakhs developing the tomb in Kaithal believed to be hers!

The popularly accepted tomb of Razia Sultana is in Bulbuli Khana, which is located behind the shrine of Baba Turkman Bayabani in then-Shahjahanabad, after which Turkman Gate is named. There is an unknown tomb next to hers. While most are of the opinion that it is that of her sister Shaziya, there are others who believe that it is her husband Altunia's—and some even claim it is actually Yakut's. No matter who is buried beside her, it was a strange occurrence for the queen of Delhi to be buried in such an inconspicuous corner on the outskirts of the city. It is said that her brother, on usurping the throne, wanted her to be buried away from the public who had truly loved the fierce and kind queen so as to avoid controversy.

There is another tomb in Kaithal district, Haryana, which is believed to be that of Razia and is a major tourist attraction there. Some say that Razia was initially interred here after her death, but was then moved to Bulbuli Khana later on.

Yet another tomb came into the limelight in 2012 at Tonk, Rajasthan, where the calligraphy reads 'Sultan Ul Hind Razia' in Arabic. The tomb has for long been referred to as 'Razia's tomb' by the locals, and the one beside hers is said to be that of Yakut. There are speculations that Razia went to Tonk after the war, which was an army camp in her father's time. This was where she died and was buried.

Needless to say, the story of this empress—inspiring in the way it broke stereotypes and rebelled against conservative traditions—is steeped in mystery. The stories of her death are as mysterious as the many lanes of Shahjahanabad, or Old Delhi, today. A rule-breaker in her life, and a legend in her death, Razia Sultana chronologically leads the pack of strong women rulers that followed in Indian history.

25

The Lost Tomb of Cleopatra

'She shall be buried by her Antony:
No grave upon the earth shall clip in it
A pair so famous.'

—Caesar in William Shakespeare's *Antony and Cleopatra*

If you go through history looking for one of the most famous, influential and beautiful queens in the world, Cleopatra is a name that will pop up. She was the last ruler of Egypt before the country became a province of the Romans in 30 BC. Her romances, her alliances, her controversial death—all of them contribute to making her a larger-than-life figure after she died.

We know enough about how the ancient emperors of Egypt were mummified and buried with vast treasures under magnificent pyramids—a major attraction for tourists from all over the world. You would think people would be lining up by the thousands to pay their tribute at the tomb of this famous queen as well. The shocking truth is that nobody knows where she was buried!

One of the greatest mysteries of Egypt, Cleopatra's lost tomb is a hot topic among Egyptologists—specialists in the scientific study of ancient Egypt. Will it ever be discovered? Where could it be located? Let's find out.

THE DEATH OF CLEOPATRA

Before we can appreciate the mystery of Cleopatra's missing tomb, we must first glance into her dramatic death that has ignited the imagination of artists and playwrights for centuries. Cleopatra fell in love with and married Mark Antony, a Roman general—which created rifts between Antony and another Roman leader, Octavius (later called

Augustus), who was also his friend and brother-in-law. You see, Antony had divorced Octavius's sister under the influence of Cleopatra; that and political differences led to Octavius declaring war on Egypt.

The Battle of Actium in Greece saw the defeat of Cleopatra and Antony, who then fled to Egypt. However, Octavius's forces later attacked their city and in the face of imminent defeat and humiliation, a historic tragedy of dramatic proportions unfolded. Cleopatra withdrew to her inner chambers and sent word to Antony that she had committed suicide, probably in an attempt to cool down Antony's anger at her, as he was her political ally and thus had also lost to Octavius. However, what she did not expect was for Antony to be so overwrought with emotion that he would stab himself in grief and die.

> **SUICIDE IN STYLE**
>
> The historian Plutarch narrates that Cleopatra's suicide ritual included a bath and a fine meal including a basket of figs.

Following this, she ultimately did commit suicide secretly with two of her handmaidens, much to the disappointment of Octavius. He wanted to take Cleopatra to Rome and parade her amidst the crowd as a symbol of his victory. He allowed Cleopatra's body to be buried along with her husband's.

CRACKS IN THE NARRATIVE

There are many versions of what actually conspired. There are historians who say that Cleopatra committed suicide by deliberately getting bitten by a snake. This is contested on the grounds that it would have been difficult to smuggle a snake into her private chambers, and even harder to get it to do as she wanted. Others say that she poisoned herself by pricking herself and injecting some poison through the wound.

Alternative theories about her suicide suggest that she did not commit suicide on her own, but was forced to do so by Octavius. He let her decide how she wanted to die. This is in direct contrast with the more popular narrative of Octavius being upset by her death as he lost the chance to display his victory fully. In fact, it is said that he even brought trained snake charmers from Libya to try and orally extract the poison from her body.

About Mark Antony, the historian Plutarch had mentioned that he was cremated, even though the search for his tomb is still in progress.

SEARCH FOR THE TOMB

Cleopatra and Antony are regarded as one of the most famous couples in history. Even William Shakespeare, the great English playwright, wrote a tragic play inspired by them, titled *Antony and Cleopatra*. The art world is filled with paintings and other work inspired by the two of them. For such a royal, romantic couple to be buried together and then to be totally lost to the world is a frustrating mystery. From what we know, their tombs are located somewhere in Alexandria in Egypt. The latest digs in Egypt in search for them were conducted by Dominican archaeologist Kathleen Martinez and Egyptologist Zahi Hawass.

> **CLEOPATRA'S COLOUR**
>
> Almost all actresses who have played the role of Queen Cleopatra were white—from Elizabeth Taylor to Angelina Jolie—although she is said to have African ethnicity.

Since 2008–09, they have been hopeful of finding the tombs in Taposiris Magna, a temple to Osiris, the god of the underworld and the judge of the dead. This temple is located to the west of Alexandria. So far, 10 mummies have been excavated from 27 tombs of the Egyptian nobility, besides yields of coins engraved with images of Cleopatra and carvings that depict her and Antony in an embrace.

Another find was an alabaster mask that had a telling cleft chin, which resembled the olden portraits we now have of Antony. Another major clue to the whereabouts of Cleopatra's tomb seems to be in an early first-century painting. It shows a rear wall that has double doors high above a woman with a crown among her handmaidens committing suicide. Found in the House of Giuseppe II in Pompeii, this has been accepted as what Cleopatra's tomb might look like—giving us an idea about the layout.

And yet the tombs continue to be out of reach of experts. The temple excavations still continue. Ground-penetrating radar revealed there was much more to discover below the surface in 2011. Italian archaeologists too have been conducting their own research into it for more than a decade—as it would be an incredible find for them, Mark Antony being 'Italian'. If we are lucky, this unbearable mystery from the annals of history might just be solved in our lifetime. All we can do is wait and watch.

26

The Disappearance of Amelia Earhart

'Women must try to do things as men have tried. When they fail, their failure must be but a challenge to others.'

—Amelia Earhart

If you haven't heard of Amelia Earhart, she is one of the most famous female aviation pioneers. If you have, you already know that she is one of the world's 'favourite missing persons'. From having quite an unladylike childhood to being one of the world's most popular American woman pilots, her life is an inspiration to women everywhere.

As she was famous in life, so she remained a legend after her death. And it is precisely her death that has made her an enigma to Americans and the world—and she continues to do so even after almost a century.

WHO WAS AMELIA EARHART?

Who was she *not*, really? Pilot, author, nurse, faculty member, career counsellor, activist—this fiery flier wore quite a number of feathers in her cap. She always broke traditional gender norms, even during her growing-up years—playing basketball and taking auto repair classes in college. Her mother did not believe in raising her daughters as 'nice little girls'—and this freedom to embrace unconventionality from childhood went a long way in moulding a young woman who was passionate about everything she did—and she always dreamt of excelling in a career that was predominantly male-dominated.

> **DID YOU KNOW?**
>
> Amelia Earhart was the sixteenth woman in the US to be issued a pilot's licence.

It was in 1920—she was 23—when she flew in a plane for the first time, and that whoosh of adrenaline cemented her ambition. 'I knew I had to fly,' she said.

ACHIEVEMENTS AND RECORDS

There was no looking back for her. She started learning from the best, practising earnestly, and it wasn't long before she, in her plane, had broken the glass ceiling to the deep blue skies above. Not only did she set multiple records, she also became a celebrity and an avowed advocate for aspiring women fliers. Earhart formed the Ninety Nines—an organization for female pilots which is still active in 44 countries. She was the first female aviator to fly solo across the Atlantic Ocean. In 1922, she flew to a height of over 14,000 feet (4.3 kilometres), setting a world record for female pilots. She bested herself in 1931, this time going over 18,000 feet (5.6 kilometres). She received many awards and accolades for her prowess, including the United States Distinguished Flying Cross. Her achievements were crucial in changing the prejudices people had about flying during that time.

> **FEMINIST FLYER**
>
> A strong advocate for women fliers, Earhart publicly refused to fly actress Mary Pickford to inaugurate an air race when it banned women from participating in the competition.

THE FLIGHT AROUND THE WORLD

It was not long before she set her eyes on the biggest goal for any professional flier at that time—to fly across the globe. Although it had been done by male pilots before, it was the first time a woman would take up this ambitious attempt. Additionally, the route she was to chart was to be the longest among any to be attempted—a whopping 29,000 miles—as she was to stick as close to the line of the equator as possible.

Her first attempt in March 1937 was a failure because of technical problems. It was her second attempt in May later that year that was bound to be successful—as she and her only crew member, Fred Noonan, had completed 22,000 miles in their Electra plane when tragedy struck.

THE DISAPPEARANCE OF AMELIA EARHART

The crew flew from Oakland, California in the US to Lae, New Guinea without much incident. However, in the middle of the flight, Earhart and Noonan lost communication with ground control. And just like that, with less than 6,000 miles of the intimidating 29,000 miles of the grand flight left, she was gone. Multiple transmissions were sent out to Earhart's plane after she stopped responding, but there was no response. There were some signals reported for four or five days after the incident, but none of it was intelligible.

THE SEARCH

Search efforts were unsuccessful. Seventeen days and $4 million later, the search was called off on 19 July, officially announcing Amelia Earhart as missing. Her husband George Putnam financed a personal search effort in the nearby islands, but that too was unsuccessful. She was legally declared dead on 5 January 1939. However, there were many reasons for people to believe that she did not really die.

> **EXPENSIVE SEARCH**
>
> At $4 million, the search for Amelia Earhart was the most expensive one undertaken by the US Navy and the Coast Guard at that time.

THE THEORIES

Crash and Sink

The most commonly accepted theory about Amelia Earhart's disappearance is that her plane ran out of fuel, crashed into the ocean, and both she and Noonan perished at sea. Experts who have studied her flight have said that it had 'poor planning, worse execution'. It is hypothesized that the flight which took off at midnight GMT must have crashed at 10 a.m. There are some who believe that the fuel tank was probably not completely filled before takeoff.

Gardner Island Hypothesis

There are alternative theories which say that Earhart, after losing contact with ground control, must have decided to look for somewhere else to land. They probably landed and survived, but were never found or killed. It is called the Gardner Island hypothesis, after the name of the island the proponents of the hypothesis believe she landed on.

Although nothing was found during the multiple searches of the piece of land, in 1940 US naval officers came across some interesting finds—a skull and bones, believed to be hers. The immediate study of the bones revealed that they belonged to a middle-aged man instead. Interestingly, further studies in 1998 showed them to be of a white woman—again negated in 2015 by another study. A sample study undertaken in 2018 theorized that the bones had more than 99 per cent possibility of being Earhart's. Rejected by the scientific community earlier, DNA testing could very well reveal the truth of it soon.

The Japanese Connection

Other theories point towards the intervention of the Japanese, who must have captured and executed the duo when they possibly crash-landed on the island of Saipan. In fact, there's even been an interview of a Saipanese woman who claimed she witnessed the execution! Photographs also made the rounds of what was claimed to be that of Noonan and Earhart after they landed. Rumours even spoke of the graves of two unknown aviators some miles away.

Some believe that the Japanese probably shot down the plane themselves. The plane was then said to be cut up and thrown into the ocean to escape discovery.

Myths and Claims

In addition to the hypotheses stated above, there were a number of other claims that were put forward. From being a spy for the US president to being a Japanese sympathizer, Earhart became a mysterious legend.

A famous claim was that her plane was discovered in the deep jungles of New Britain.

Controversy erupted when one author in his book claimed that Amelia Earhart changed her identity after safely surviving the flight and moved to New Jersey, becoming one Irene Craigmile Bolam.

LEGACY

The mystery of Amelia Earhart's disappearance continues to haunt the popular psyche. The flight she died trying to complete was later undertaken by other female pilots to commemorate her. During her life, she inspired an entire generation of female pilots. In her death, she continues to be an icon for generations to come.

27

The Disappearance of Agatha Christie

'Very few of us are what we seem.'

—Agatha Christie

What happens when the most upcoming and increasingly popular crime novelist of the era suddenly goes missing—not for one, or two, but 11 days? When a master of the written word—who excelled in creating plots of intriguing whodunnits—herself goes down the rabbit hole of a real-life mystery? What happens is that one of the strangest and most memorable mysteries in the realm of literature takes place. Or, as renowned litterateur Oscar Wilde once said, 'Life imitates art far more than art imitates life.'

This is the real story of Agatha Christie and how she went missing—triggering one of the biggest manhunts of her time.

WHO IS AGATHA CHRISTIE?

There are very few bookworms who have not picked up at least one Agatha Christie novel in their lives, fewer still who have not heard of her. Probably the first most famous English crime novelist in the world after Arthur Conan Doyle, Christie's work continues to spellbind all readers who come across it—with its confounding mysteries and titillating clues.

She began her career as a writer in the early twentieth century, with her first novel published in 1920. With dozens of detective novels, short story collections and romances, she has been recognized by the Guinness World Records as one of the best-selling novelists of all time. In fact, her books apparently come third only to the Bible and William Shakespeare's works in terms of being the most published books of the world.

She was married to an army man Archibald Christie for 12 years before he asked her for a divorce. He had fallen in love with his 25-year-old secretary Nancy Neele and thus wanted to end his marriage. It was a cold night in December 1926 when Christie disappeared, following a fight with her husband before he left the house to spend the weekend with his mistress. What followed after was to grasp the imagination of the public for years to come.

THE DISAPPEARANCE

The known facts were that on the evening of 3 December, after her husband left, Christie had dinner and went upstairs to kiss their seven-year-old daughter Rosalind goodbye. She left the house at 9:45 p.m., leaving behind a letter for her secretary. She mentioned in the letter that she was going to Yorkshire, some 300 kilometres from their Berkshire home. The next morning, her car, which seemed to have been in an accident, was found near a chalk quarry. The headlights were still on. Her driving licence and coat were still inside. But there was no trace of the person. The uproar that followed was not surprising.

> **BIGGEST (WO)MANHUNT**
>
> The search for her was one of the largest of that time—with over 1,000 policemen, 15,000 volunteers and a number of aeroplanes. In fact, this was one of the first times that planes were being used to search for a missing person.

Her husband became the prime suspect of the investigators. It only added to the suspense that her car was found near a local lake infamously named Silent Pool where two young children had died before. She too was believed to have drowned, among a number of lurid theories that sprang up. But her body was not found.

Her disappearance made front page news. Newspapers were offering rewards to help find her. Other famous writers of that time, such as Arthur Conan Doyle and Dorothy L. Sayers, also became involved. In fact, Doyle—who had great faith in psychics—gave one of Christie's gloves to a clairvoyant to help locate her. The irony was not lost on anyone—a mystery writer who seemed to have literally walked into a mystery herself!

It was on the eleventh day that the novelist was found at the Old Swan Hotel (then called the Swan Hydropathic Hotel) in Yorkshire, after hotel authorities informed the police that she was there under a different name. If you thought this was the end to the mystery, sit tight—we have only got started.

Firstly, Christie seemed to have signed in at the hotel under the surname of her husband's girlfriend, Theresa Neele. Secondly, she seemed to have absolutely no recollection of how she had ended up there or what had happened to her! In fact, she apparently had a look of puzzlement when her husband went up to her in the hotel dining room where she was seated. Needless to say, as the saying goes, the truth was getting way stranger than fiction.

WHAT ACTUALLY HAPPENED?

These 11 days of her disappearance sparked the imagination of the general public and experts alike. Given that either Christie could not or did not reveal any further information about her actions, the incident became a grand blank canvas for everyone to paint out their theories.

The public opined that this was either a publicity stunt to promote her new book or an attempt by her to frame her husband out of jealousy. However, psychologists who had examined her reported that she had suffered amnesia following a concussion when her car had an accident on the way. She had taken a train and arrived at the hotel without any luggage. It seemed that her work, her mother's death and her husband's infidelity had all culminated to cause depression, insomnia and possibly a nervous breakdown.

Interestingly, author Andrew Wilson has posited a new theory that following the incident Christie had

> **MEMORY LOST, NEW IDENTITY CREATED**
>
> Her psychological trance apparently caused her to adopt a new personality as Theresa Neele, and she could not recognize herself when she read the news about the disappearance of Agatha Christie in newspapers!

probably planned to commit suicide when she had left home. He wrote about this in his book, *A Talent for Murder*. He drew his hypothesis from the books she had written under a pseudonym. Besides, in a lone interview she gave to a newspaper, she had spoken of the fateful incident—how she had wanted to drive her car into the quarry earlier that day, but decided against it as she had her daughter with her at the time. Later that night, she left 'with the intention of doing something desperate'. However, she couldn't go through with it and invented the story of amnesia out of embarrassment.

THE AFTERMATH

Agatha Christie and her husband did end up getting divorced, and he finally married his mistress. And Christie never spoke of those 11 days again, not even in her extensive autobiography. It was left to others to weave fictional books and make movies about the incident—which were controversial, to say the least. In fact, the movie *Agatha* in 1979 was highly denounced by her daughter Rosalind Hicks, for maligning the memory of her mother. She even went to court against it, but it was released without any hiccups.

It has been around a century since the disappearance, but it continues to spellbind Agatha Christie fans and mystery lovers alike. After all, this was the greatest mystery the author ever created.

HISTORY'S TREASURES

28

Who Stole the Irish Crown Jewels?

'If you don't get caught, you deserve everything you steal.'

—Daniel Nayeri

If only it were as simple as that! Opulence, scandal, secrets and accusations—the case of the missing Irish Crown Jewels is one of the most enduring mysteries of Ireland. Long before there were heist movies that kept us on the edge of our seats, there were already jewels worth millions being stolen by nifty criminals. And like most of the fictional movies, the real-life thief of the Irish Crown Jewels was never really caught and punished. More than a century since the grand theft, it still makes for an engrossing read.

WHAT ARE THE IRISH CROWN JEWELS?

The actual name of these stolen jewels is the 'Jewels Belonging to the Most Illustrious Order of Saint Patrick', also called the State Jewels of Ireland. They include a star and a badge worn by the heads of the Order. The original regalia was quite ordinary when the Order was established in 1783.

It was almost 80 years later that these were replaced by the king. The stones were taken from royal ornaments and assembled by one of the best jewellers of the era. Both were heavily jewelled—the star containing a whopping 394 precious stones!

It was made with the purest Brazilian diamonds and had a cross of rubies and a trefoil of emeralds. This surrounded a circle of sky blue enamel, inside which the year 1783 was engraved in Roman in rose diamonds. This glittering star would have been worth almost £1.5 million in 2018.

The badge was oval with almost the same design as the star. However, it was surrounded by a circle of large and pure Brazilian diamonds, over which was a harp and a loop engraved in similar diamonds. This blinding piece of regalia would have set a collector back by nearly £1.7 million in 2018.

Together, both of them are estimated to be worth over £3 million today.

But that's not all. Along with these two regalia, collars of five Knight Members of the Order were also stolen. Together, these were valued at over a thousand pounds at the time of the theft.

THE INCIDENT

It all started when a new safe was constructed in 1903 to store the jewels securely. The safe would have been placed inside a new vault constructed in Dublin Castle, which was beside the office of Sir Arthur Vicars, a senior military officer. Since it would not fit in the vault, the safe was stored inside Vicars's office and he had the responsibility of looking after the keys to the safe, while the keys to his office were held by both Vicars and his staff. All was well for four years.

It was on 6 July 1907, just four days before the visit of the king and the queen, that the jewels were discovered to be missing! The cleaner of the building had found the doors open—as he had on a number of occasions—and even come across an intruder in the vault once. Since there was no sign of a forced entrance, it was understood to have been an inside job.

The royalty was angered, the police got on the case while psychics had strange visions of the location of the jewels. There were rumours, theories, accusations and denials, making it one of the most sensational heists in the history of Ireland.

Was Vicars to blame? Whether he had stolen the jewels or not, he had certainly given rise to a lot of talk, as he was an alcoholic who used to get drunk regularly on night duty. In fact, in the middle of one such drunken night, he had apparently woken up to find the jewels around his neck!

THE INVESTIGATION

Instead of the matter clearing up, things started getting even murkier once the police began their investigation. This was because the report submitted by Scotland Yard detective John Kane—in which he apparently named the culprit—was never allowed to be released by the Irish police force. In the meantime, Vicars was under the limelight but refused to both resign from his position as well as appear before a commission looking into the theft.

> **THE SHERLOCK HOLMES CONNECTION**
>
> Sir Arthur Conan Doyle was a distant cousin of Sir Arthur Vicars, and offered to help in the investigation of the theft.

What Vicars did, though, was publicly accuse Francis Shackleton, his next-in-command, of the crime. Shackleton was defended by Kane as he was not in the country when the incident occurred, and Vicars was ultimately forced to resign.

THE SPECULATIONS

When there is not a single person arrested after such an infamous theft, rumours and suppositions flow naturally. There were many accusations being made at political groups and military figures of that time; for instance, the secret organization Irish Republican Brotherhood was believed to have smuggled the jewels to the US.

Another theory is that this theft was a ploy by an opposition political group to humiliate the then ruling Liberal government. It is said that they gave back the jewels to the royal family once the storm of controversy had blown over.

One of the most enduring theories that was put forward in the 1960s was that the actual incident of the theft had to be kept under wraps to avoid bringing into open greater scandals that occurred within the walls of the Office of the Arms. Apparently Shackleton was the mastermind behind the heist after all, but in cahoots with one Captain Richard Gorges. Both of them were homosexuals—which was a crime under Irish law at that time. It is believed Gorges got Arthur Vicars very drunk one night, took his keys to the safe, and stole the jewels. They were then apparently smuggled to Amsterdam by Shackleton later.

Such debauchery in a senior authority's office was not something the Irish government wanted to make public. It was to avoid a witch-hunt that the investigating commission was set up—in an attempt to whitewash the occurrence and to sweep the more scandalous truths under the carpet.

> **FINAL SUSPECT A THIEF AFTER ALL**
>
> The final suspect in the crime was one Francis Goldney, who had joined work at the Dublin Castle a few months before the theft. On his death in 1918, a trove of stolen goods was discovered in his home. However, the jewels were never found.

THE ACTUAL CULPRIT

To this day, there has been no one officially accused of this fascinating crime. The jewels have probably long been broken apart and sold individually, or they must be part of some rich collector's possessions, or hidden away and forgotten somewhere. The only thing that remains is the sheer mystery of it all—and will probably stay so for all time to come.

29

The Missing Peacock Throne

'History has remembered the kings and warriors, because they destroyed; art has remembered the people, because they created.'

—William Morris

And yet, what of kings and emperors who were patrons of art and culture and commissioned wondrous works whose magnificence shines through the corridors of history? One such king was Shah Jahan who we already admire for his brilliant marble mausoleum, the Taj Mahal in Agra. Considered one of the modern seven wonders of the world, it is still not the most opulent thing the Mughal emperor commissioned during his reign.

We're talking about the grandiose Peacock Throne—the most expensive throne ever made in the world. Read on to find out just how costly Shah Jahan's throne was.

THE TAKHT-E-MURASSA

Long before historians started calling it the Peacock Throne, it was known simply as the Jewelled or Ornamented Throne or the Takht-e-Murassa. That was probably the only thing simple about it. Built over a period of seven years by Mughal master goldsmith Said Gilani and the imperial craftsmen, it was inaugurated on the

> **A KING IS KNOWN BY THE THRONE HE BUILDS!**
>
> Not all Mughal kings shared Shah Jahan's love for opulence. His father Jehangir's throne was a stark contrast to the Peacock Throne—an imposing rectangular slab of black onyx imported from Belgium. When the British had attacked, a cannonball had struck the throne, caused only a slight crack on one side, and then bounced off!

seventh anniversary of Shah Jahan's ascension, on 22 March 1635. Astrologers fixed that date for the inauguration as both Eid-ul-Fitr and Nowruz coincided on this day.

The gilded throne was over 6 feet long and 4 feet wide, with a height of around 15 feet. The canopy featured peacocks on it, which is why it was later called the Peacock Throne. Thick-set with jewels, this imposing seat was a true symbol of the Golden Age of the Mughal Empire in India. In fact, it has been compared to the Takht-e-Suleman or the Throne of Solomon. Shah Jahan was called Zille-e-Illahi, or Shadow of God on Earth, so it is only fitting that his throne was as extravagant as his title.

The throne was placed in the Diwan-i-Khas of the Red Fort, where the emperor received foreign dignitaries, select courtiers and aristocrats, although it is said that it was later moved to the Diwan-e-Aam where he held court for a wider public.

THE MAKING OF THE THRONE

The magnificence of this throne is unparalleled in history; it was wrought out of 1,150 kilograms of gold and studded with precious stones weighing 230 kilograms. This included gems such as diamonds, rubies, garnets, sapphires, emeralds and pearls.

The jewels that went into the making of the Peacock Throne come with their own identity and legacy. Some of these are:

The Koh-i-Noor Diamond (186 carats)

Originally acquired by Allaudin Khilji, it is one of the largest-cut diamonds in the world that is now in the possession of the British Crown.

The Akbar Shah Diamond (73 carats)

Belonging to Akbar, it was supposedly set as one of the eyes of the peacocks on the throne. It is now probably in the possession of the royal Gaekwad family of Baroda.

The Shah Diamond (88.7 carats)

Seized by Akbar, it is today part of the Moscow Kremlin.

The Timur Ruby (361 carats)

Also called the Khiraj-i-Alam or Tribute to the World, it was seized along with the Koh-i-Noor from Duleep Singh, the last maharaja of the Sikh Empire, and now belongs to the British Crown. It is the second-largest spinel ruby in the world.

> **SIZE DOES NOT MATTER**
>
> The Taj Mahal might be an epic monument, but did you know it cost less to construct it than it did to build the Peacock Throne? That's correct! It apparently cost twice as much at that time.

It was not just the throne that was splendid; the cost borne by Shah Jahan for the craftsmanship was also exorbitant. Gilani, the goldsmith, was paid with gold coins equal to his weight for his craftsmanship. Poet Abu Talib Kalim was paid for his 63 couplets for the throne with six gold pieces for each verse. Shah Jahan's favourite poet, Mohammad Qudsi, composed 20 verses that were inscribed on the throne in emerald and green enamel.

THE INVASION, THE LOOT AND THE LOSS

When the Persian ruler Nadir Shah invaded India in 1739, he made off with loot that would have amounted to $5 billion in today's time—and the Peacock Throne was sadly part of that, as were many other jewels and cultural artefacts. Nadir Shah stopped taxation for three years after the plunder, so great was his loot.

However, what goes around comes around. It was in 1747 that Nadir Shah was assassinated by his own officials. What ensued was a complete state of chaos. In this uproar, the 'costliest treasure in history' went missing, believed to have been dismantled by Persian tribesmen, and parts of it hidden away, sold off or destroyed. Today, there is no trace of the Peacock Throne, except a number of rumours:

1. The throne was given to the Ottoman Sultan as a gift.
2. Part of it was used to build the Sun Throne commissioned by the Persian emperor Fath-Ali Shah in the early nineteenth century. Its platform was similar in shape to the Peacock Throne, but there is no evidence to back up the rumours.
3. A Sikh legend claims that a rectangular stone slab said to be part of the throne was uprooted and brought to Amritsar by one Jassa Singh Ramgarhia as war booty. It has never been corroborated independently by historians and scientists.
4. The director of New York's Metropolitan Museum of Art purported to have obtained a marble leg in 1908 from the pedestal of the throne. Another marble leg is known to be displayed in the Victoria and Albert Museum in London. It is unclear if they really belonged to the throne, and if not, then what their origin is.
5. Another rumour goes that the legs of the 1836 Qajar Throne of Iran, also called the Peacock Throne, was taken from the original throne.

THE AFTERMATH

Bereft of the glittering glory of the Peacock Throne, a replacement was built—less grand than the original. Unfortunately, this too went missing after the Indian Rebellion of 1857 broke out. However, it was not the last to be made. Several other thrones in history were inspired by the original—one of which was the Bavarian King Ludwig II's version in the Linderhof Palace.

The mystery of the disappearance of the world's costliest throne pales in comparison to the sheer tragedy of its loss. Valued at $804 million in 1999, it would be worth a whopping $1.24 billion in 2019 when adjusted for inflation. And all we have to remember it by are the jewels that now belong to other countries—and a few paintings of the replacement throne.

30

The Legend of the Missing Nazi Gold

'Imagine if gold turned into lead when stolen.'

—Satoshi Nakamoto

Going by this quote, one of the things that would certainly happen is that Adolf Hitler would have been an insignificant name in the history of Europe and Germany would have lost a lot sooner during World War II. The entire war was carried out by Nazi Germany with weapons and goods bought from neutral countries with robbed gold. In fact, experts have called it history's greatest robbery.

So how much gold did Adolf Hitler's government capture? Almost $600 million, which, in today's time, would be worth over $19 billion. Interestingly, all this gold as well as other valuables and assets were never completely recovered after the war.

And that is what is the most fascinating part of this chapter from history: where did all the gold go?

THE BEGINNING

There are few people who would not know of the role Nazi Germany played during World War II, fewer still who would not have heard of Adolf Hitler. Aided by his finance minister and army, Hitler managed to empty the banks of Austria, erstwhile Czechoslovakia, Poland, Belgium and the Netherlands. The Swiss banks are believed to have assisted in laundering this loot. It helped the German dictator keep his wartime activities running smoothly without a hiccup.

After their first seizure in Austria, most European countries wanted to avoid such a fate. To avoid getting plundered by Germany, they sent their gold for safekeeping to Canada and the US. Even the Vatican and the Soviet Union did the same.

While the gold stolen from the countries' central banks account for around $600 million, it does not account for the assets stolen from private companies and individuals—thus leaving the total value of their assets still unclear, as of today.

This has been a fascinating topic discussed in many books and conspiracy theories.

THE SECRET STASHES AND DENIALS

> **AND THE GOLD WENT TO...**
>
> Despite all the mystery, it is estimated that nearly 100 tons of gold was laundered through Swiss banks. Out of this, only 4 tons were returned at the end of the war. After Switzerland, Portugal was the second largest receiver of Nazi gold. This was in exchange for tungsten, a metal required for producing ammunitions that the Germans did not have.

It was in 1945 when the US army advanced to Germany and discovered one of their biggest loots at Kaiseroda salt mine in Merkers. Inside a vault room in the mines were 8,307 gold bars, 3,682 cartons of German currency, 3,326 bags of gold coins, 207 containers of Nazi loot, including valuable artwork, 80 bags of foreign currency, 63 bags of silver, 55 boxes of gold bullion, eight bags of gold rings and one bag of platinum bars.

During the war, the Swiss National Bank is said to have received $440 million of Nazi gold, out of which $316 million is guessed to

> **THE DEEP-SEA TREASURES**
>
> In 2017, the German cargo ship *SS Minden* which sunk in 1939 was discovered. Nazi gold worth $130 million was believed to have been on board the vessel. However, a lot of explorations and undersea hunts later, it was discovered that there's no gold there.

have been looted. By the end of World War II, Germany still had $300 million in gold—more than what it had when it started.

A top secret American report—made public in 1997—revealed that the Vatican had confiscated $350 million of Nazi gold in 1945. Of this, $150 million was seized by the British, and the rest was transferred to Vatican City. The Vatican Bank continues to deny this.

In fact, a civil lawsuit was filed against them in 2000, which was later dismissed.

THE GOLD TRAIN

This mystery of the remaining Nazi gold culminates at present in the legend of the Nazi gold train. It is believed that the Germans, in January 1945, hid a train filled with gold and other valuables in a tunnel in south-west Poland which was then part of Germany. Many searches have been conducted in the area since then by archaeologists, treasure hunters and other experts, but nothing has been found. Between 1947 and 1989, the Polish Armed Forces carried out searches. The hype around the legend lulled after that, until 2015, when it caught the attention of treasure seekers worldwide.

Two men claimed to have obtained the exact location of the gold train from a dying World War II survivor, and even shared ground-penetrating radar images as proof. But after hundreds of thousands of dollars, numerous man-hours and a worldwide sensation, nothing was eventually found. The images were revealed to be those of natural icicle formations, although they looked like train carriages.

But the search continues. After all, rumour has it that this hidden train holds up to 300 tons of gold, besides precious stones, weapons and artwork!

MYSTERIOUS PLACES

31

What Happened in the Cursed Village of Kuldhara?

'Ever since the world began, it has been the belief of mankind that desolate places are the special haunt of supernatural beings.'

—Richard Jefferies

There is a perverse pleasure in spooking ourselves out with ghost stories, regardless of how old we get. And if you are among the few people who want to experience it first-hand, there are a number of places in India for your bucket list—one of the most interesting being the cursed village of Kuldhara. A topic of much fascination among paranormal experts, it is said to have been cursed by the villagers before they apparently abandoned it overnight. With the curse in place, it has been reduced to a ghost town and no one's been able to reside in it since then.

THE GHOST VILLAGE

Located in the sprawling district of Jaisalmer in Rajasthan, Kuldhara was once a thriving village established in the thirteenth century by the Paliwal brahmins. It was a small township built around the temple of a mother goddess. In the early nineteenth century, the villagers supposedly left—and no one knows exactly why. And it was not just Kuldhara—83 villages in

> **THE MYSTERIOUS TUNNELS**
>
> Oral history tells us about how the villagers disappeared in the middle of the night through a tunnel. Around 100 tunnels are said to have been found under the villages, although no one has explored them enough to find out where they end. Local legends say they open up in Egypt and Afghanistan, but that's for adventurers to explore.

Jaisalmer became 'ghost towns'. What has trickled down from those times are oral histories and local legends.

Today, this village lies desolate and quiet—an abandoned site that has captured the imagination of tourists and media alike.

REASONS FOR ABANDONMENT

Dwindling Water Supply

A survey of the village has revealed that it was probably lack of water that caused the villagers to leave. Scarcity of water would have caused difficulties in cultivation, and taxation on the villagers would have added to their woes. In the 1990s, the only water found there was stagnant water in parts of the dried-up riverbed.

Going by the population estimates over the centuries, the abandonment seems to have been in phases. The populace figures at around 1,588 in the seventeenth and eighteenth centuries, which dwindled to 800 in 1815. By then, some settlers had already deserted the village. In 1890, the population record showed 37 people.

Shaky Grounds

A 2017 study has revealed that it could have been caused by an earthquake. The ruined houses show signs of destruction that are commonly attributed to earthquakes and not to the wear and tear caused by time. The collapsed roofs and fallen pillars have been connected to tectonic activities in the region.

The Evil Minister

The minister of Jaisalmer state, Salim Singh, occupies an especially hateful place in the hearts of Jaisalmer residents. He did not just impose high taxes on the villagers, but would not even relax the taxes when agricultural produce was affected due to less water supply. He was said to have been a lecherous official who eyed the Paliwal women. He seems to have had a major role in the abandonment of the village.

The Final Straw

The villagers had had enough when Salim Singh demanded a nine-year-old Brahmin girl's hand in marriage and gave them 10 days to comply. The girl was probably the village chief's daughter, and they would never give her away to a man of lower caste. So, as nearby locals would probably have been able to tell you, all the residents of the 84 villages quietly disappeared in the dead of night. Till date, no one knows where they went or resettled.

> **HAUNTED TREASURES**
>
> It is said that since the Paliwals had to leave suddenly at night without much that would weigh them down, they buried their treasures underground. They hoped to one day come and collect it. This was proven true when a gang of thieves were arrested for stealing 1 kilogram of silver and 150 grams of gold from the ruins in 2018. There are possibilities of more such valuables buried in the Kuldhara ruins.

PARANORMAL ACTIVITIES

The village is today maintained by the ASI as a heritage site. An eerie expanse of ruins, it can give even the bravest of us a tingle along the spine, especially at night. It is said that since the Paliwals cursed the village as they left, there have been mysterious sudden deaths and rare births here. According to legend, so powerful was this curse that it attracted evil spirits that reside there even today. Some say that no one can spend an entire night there without getting killed or losing their mind.

The interesting thing is, in the 2010s, Gaurav Tiwari of the Indian Paranormal Society spent the night at this site with his team and TV crew. Bizarre experiences and inexplicable sightings were reported, and these fuelled interest in the village. Tiwari died a few years later under mysterious circumstances in his bathroom.

Today, Kuldhara village is considered one of the most haunted places in India and no one is allowed to visit it at night. If you were ever to visit Jaisalmer, this would be a great stop if you are not faint-hearted. A desolate tourist spot, it evokes a strange hollowness in the pit of your stomach as you survey the ruins.

32

Who Destroyed the Library of Alexandria?

'The real tragedy of the Library at Alexandria was not that the incendiaries burned immensely, but that they had neither the leisure nor the taste to discriminate.'

—Arthur Quiller-Couch

Today, like everyone else, bookworms too have gone digital. From ebooks to audiobooks, the old-school style of buying actual books or going to public libraries is not the only way to consume knowledge and literature anymore. Nowadays, all you have to do is tap your mobile screens a few times to have all the information you want in front of your eyes in a matter of seconds. However, things weren't so convenient in the ancient times. In fact, way back in the third century BC, there was no conceivable way for multiple copies of books to be made without actually copying it painstakingly by hand.

So, you would understand how revered a library at that time would be, especially if it had around 40,000 to 400,000 scrolls on varied subjects under the sky. That was the grandeur of the Library of Alexandria—one of the largest and most famous in the world at that time—tragically destroyed, and its wealth of knowledge lost to generations that followed.

Only bibliophiles who know the pain of lending their books—for fear of damage, or worse, never getting them back—would comprehend the immensity of this loss.

THE HISTORY OF THE LIBRARY

Located in Alexandria, Egypt, it was not an independent library but part of a bigger institute for research called the Mouseion built between 285 BC and 246 BC, it was dedicated to the nine goddesses of the arts. Alexandria soon came to be known as the capital of knowledge and learning, thanks to this great library, where over 100 scholars were employed at its most fruitful period.

> **THE OLDEST LIBRARIES IN THE WORLD**
>
> Although the Library of Alexandria is one of the most famous from the ancient times, it is not the oldest in the world. The earliest record of archived written materials goes back to 3400 BC in Uruk in the Sumerian Civilization. The oldest library that no longer exists is the Library of Ashurbanipal in Nineveh, Iraq, founded in the seventh century BC.

The rulers of that period followed an aggressive policy to ensure that the library was the fountain of all knowledge. They used to send out royal agents with abundant money to purchase books, regardless of subject and author, although older texts were given more priority. In fact, if required, they would collect the original books, copy them out and then return the copies to the owners.

It flowered into a hub of knowledge and new ideas with time. In fact, the system of organizing books alphabetically first started here. Zoology, literature, mathematics, geography, medicine, literary criticism and many other subjects were developed under the intellectual pursuits of the scholars during the peak period of the library.

DECLINE AND DESTRUCTION

After over a century of stimulating intellectual development, the library entered the stage of inevitable decline. It first started when there was a power struggle between the seventh and eighth Ptolemaic kings, with the latter murdering the former and expelling all foreign scholars and causing the head librarian to also flee. The Mouseion lost its authority as scholars and their students began to carry out independent research and establish separate schools.

Julius Caesar's Burning of the Library

In 48 BC, during the Great Roman Civil War, Julius Caesar was besieged at Alexandria and outnumbered by the enemy fleet. He ordered his own ships to be set on fire, which soon engulfed the enemy ships too. However, the damage also spread to the dock and the buildings nearby, which included the Library of Alexandria. Some historians have pointed out that around 40,000 scrolls were destroyed in this fire—a great travesty the library would have found it hard to recover from. Interestingly, Julius Caesar himself, as well as a few other noted historians, have not mentioned any damage to the library during this fire.

> **THE GIFT OF LOVE...OR 200,000 SCROLLS!**
>
> While Cleopatra's former lover Julius Caesar apparently was the first to destroy the library, it was Caesar's trusted general and her husband Mark Antony who is said to have given her all 200,000 scrolls from the Library of Pergamum in Turkey to make up for the loss! Now that's a gift that would make any book lover starry-eyed.

Destruction During the Roman Period

Since then to the third century BC—during the Roman rule—the state of affairs in both Alexandria as well as the library declined. Its fall in reputation was marked by the rise in that of other libraries across the Mediterranean region as well as in the city itself—one of which was the Serapeum, a temple to the Graeco-Egyptian god Serapis, which was built as a daughter library to the main one.

Another battle during this period between Emperor Aurelian and Palmyrene Queen Zenobia in AD 272 destroyed the part of the city in which the library was located. If anything survived, it must have been destroyed during another siege in 297.

The Attack of the Christians

The Serapeum itself was not to be. In the fourth century, with the rise of Christianity, the bishop of Alexandria, Theophilus, angered the city's people with his mocking parade of its ancient cult objects. This led to a guerrilla attack by the teachers and students of the Serapeum on the Christians. This resulted in a counter-attack that destroyed the daughter library.

The Final Blow by the Muslim Conquest

In the seventh century, when the Muslim army came to capture Alexandria, they had already heard of 'a great library' there. The caliph Omar is said to have ordered to destroy all books—as they were 'useless', whether they were in agreement with the Quran, or against it.

THE GREAT LIBRARY'S LEGACY

The phases in which the library was destroyed, rebuilt and finally erased from history forever are a mystery. Located in the heart of a volatile nation where pagans, Christians, Jews and Muslims fought each other, it was a fragile jewel never destined to last.

However, its legacy survived with a number of Christian libraries modelled directly after it during the Roman Empire's rise. Today, the Bibliotheca Alexandrina is a modern library in Alexandria that has been built to commemorate the ancient institute. It is the result of a joint project by Egypt and the UN.

33

Why Is No One Allowed on North Sentinel Island?

'Things forbidden have a secret charm.'

—Tacitus

If you were allowed to go anywhere in a park, except one dark corner for your own safety, what would your reaction be? If you thought to secretly explore the forbidden corner, you are no different from the average human being. We crave the excitement of new and forbidden discoveries.

And yet, there are those that neither want to discover nor be discovered. While the world is already embracing 5G technology and missions to Mars, these reclusive groups are literally stuck in the Stone Age, making do with the most basic survival skills.

Yes! They are called 'uncontacted people' and there are over a 100 of them across the world. From the dense forests of South America and New Guinea to the Andaman and Nicobar Islands, these isolated people stay away from all human civilization in tight-knit groups and are a source of curiosity for the outside world.

But like they say, curiosity killed the cat, and trying to get too close to them can sometimes lead to misadventures, for instance, death. And that is why absolutely no one is allowed on the North Sentinel Island, one of the islands of the Andaman cluster of islands, which is home to the most secluded tribe of the world, the Sentinelese.

WHO ARE THEY?

It is ironic that India, the second most populated country in the world where people have to jostle for space in all public spaces, is home to one of the most famous uncontacted tribes of the world! How long they have been living on North Sentinel Island is not certain; while some say they have been there for 60,000 years, other experts believe that they deliberately migrated there recently or when their 60 square kilometre island drifted away from another, Little Andaman. Their first recorded sighting was almost 250 years ago, in 1771.

Short, dark and mostly naked, the Sentinelese number anything between 80 and 100, according to anthropologists. While they share certain similarities with other tribes of the island state such as the Jarawi and the Onge, they are the most reclusive. In fact, even the Indian authorities leave them alone.

Despite being aloof from civilization, technology and even agriculture, they can fend for themselves pretty well. Hunter-gatherers, they also catch local seafood and include wild fruits and raw honey in their diet. They live in temporary huts made from branches and leaves, and know the use of fire as well as the value of metal for their tools and weapons.

> **TOO GOOD AT GOODBYES!**
>
> Photos of the Sentinelese people might show them as mostly violent—with bows and arrows or spears. However, they have other, less hostile ways of expressing their displeasure at outsiders who seek to make contact. They turn their backs and squat down as if they are defecating—a sign to the onlooker that they are not welcome.

Their reclusiveness has kept them away from many contagious diseases, which would certainly kill them if they were exposed to the outside world. But what did not kill them was the deadly earthquake and tsunami that struck the Indian Ocean in 2004. Almost 2.5 lakh people died in the tragedy, but when helicopters went near their island three days later to survey the damage, the gritty Sentinelese were still alive and kicking. In fact, they attacked the choppers with their arrows and spears!

ARE THEY DANGEROUS?

And this brings us to the menacing mystery of this tribe. While experts who have managed to make contact with them over the years are of the belief that they are not hostile, the Sentinelese certainly have a record of violence that would intimidate any curious explorer. The latest to find it out the hard way was an American missionary who was killed by them in 2018. John Allen Chau paid Andamanese fishermen to take him to the island—in flagrant violation of the Indian law that prohibits anyone from getting closer than 5 nautical miles to the island.

Even before this, they had killed two fishermen in 2006 who had unknowingly sailed too close to the island. History tells us of shipwrecked survivors fending off attacks by the Sentinelese time and again before being rescued. A convict once escaped to the island in 1896, only to have his throat cut and body pierced with their arrows. His body was found later. Three years later, some more fugitives to the island were found to have been killed by this secluded group.

The Indian Navy patrols the surroundings to ensure such incidents are not repeated in future. Even if they are, the Sentinelese people are not prosecuted for killing people who come from other places. They are protected by law. Clearly, this tribe wants to be left alone, in peace. Whether we should let them is another debate altogether.

ARE THEY REALLY UNCONTACTED?

So, if the Sentinelese people are truly one of the last of the uncontacted tribes of the world, how do we know so much about them? The answer is that because they have been contacted. There have been a number of explorers curious to learn more about their lives and customs ever since they were first sighted.

During the time of the British, it was a naval officer, Maurice Vidal Portman, who travelled to the island multiple times in the 1880s. His experiences with the tribe were not pleasant—as was to be expected. On one of his visits, he kidnapped six of them and brought them to the mainland. The two elderly ones became sick and died soon after. He sent the remaining four—all children—back with gifts.

Since then, they were pretty much left alone till the 1960s, when the Indian government attempted to make contact with the tribe by sending teams every few years. The most famous name among those is Triloknath Pandit of the ASI, who was one of the first to make peaceful contact with the Sentinelese. He continued to go with his team bearing gifts, and it was a milestone in the history of contacting this secluded tribe when the islanders did not display open hostility to them. Not only was he allowed to enter their village, but they also conversed with him in an unknown tongue from afar.

> **DID ONE MAN'S OBSESSION SCAR THE SENTINELESE FOREVER?**
>
> Maurice Vidal Portman apparently developed an unhealthy obsession with the Sentinelese and used to measure their bodies and take photographs. According to a human rights organization campaigning for tribal rights, these antics probably caused the tribe to become hostile to and wary of outsiders for generations after—even today.

They accepted the gifts of coconuts from the hands of T.N. Pandit's team in 1991—a major breakthrough. However, when they tried to bring other tribes' people to help in translation, all camaraderie was severed as the Sentinelese became visibly angry. Today, no more contact is made—the 100-odd people are left to their own devices.

Do they even know what lies out there, in this big vast world? Do they care? Will they ever join civilization or forever remain reclusive—whether they flourish or perish? These are mysteries, finding the answers to which can cost lives. All we can do is wonder.

34

The Tragic Mystery of Malcha Mahal

'Ordinariness is not just a crime; it is a sin.'

—Princess Sakina Mahal

Deep in the Ridge Forest of Delhi lies a monument swathed in mystery and tragedy. To the uninitiated, it is just a Mughal-era hunting lodge built by Firoz Shah Tughlaq that lies decrepit and uninhabited, next to the Delhi Earth Station run by the Indian Space Research Organization (ISRO). But the story behind this structure certainly deserves a retelling.

THE PALACE

The monument is called Malcha Mahal—or Wilayat Mahal—and came under the ownership of Awadh's Begum Wilayat Mahal in 1985 after a long and tenuous protest by her against the then Indira Gandhi government. Self-proclaimed descendant of Wajid Ali Shah, the last Nawab of Awadh, Begum Mahal demanded that she be paid reparations for her lost ancestral property after the British seized them all when Shah's kingdom was annexed. She wanted the Indian government to recognize the contributions of the Kingdom of Awadh—which is part of modern-day Uttar Pradesh—in the revolution of 1857 against the British.

> **WHO LET THE DOGS OUT?**
>
> Begum Wilayat Mahal was famous for her cold manner—and she once let her vicious bloodhounds loose on a politician when he was still a kid. His fault? The fact that he approached her! Later, her kids too would be infamous for threatening to set dogs on any unwanted visitors to their decrepit mansion.

THE PROTEST

Begun Wilayat Mahal had an eccentric personality. Stern and tenacious, she held a protest camp in the 1970s at the first-class waiting room of the New Delhi Railway Station—along with her seven servants, her son Cyrus and daughter Sakina, and around 15 fierce bloodhounds. Her unrelenting power move finally chipped away at the government's inaction—and almost a decade later in 1985, she was given ownership of Malcha Mahal.

THE PRIDE

Hidden away deep inside the Ridge area of Delhi, the Mahal had neither doors nor windows nor electricity nor running water, but wide-open arches. And yet the proud Mahal family laid claim to it in their regal manner: putting up a huge metal sign that warned intruders to keep away or face the wrath of their dogs and guns.

However, difficult times were not over for these last three members of the royal family of Awadh, isolated in their ancient mahal in the woods. Begum Wilayat Mahal, after enjoying eight years of living in her victory mansion, finally succumbed to what must have been a long spell of depression. And her suicide is no less legendary than the historic deaths of queens across the world—including Cleopatra, who is said to have died of snakebite.

Apparently, Begum Mahal crushed all the diamonds from the last few items of jewellery she was left with and swallowed them!

THE PROGENY

After her death, Prince Cyrus and Princess Sakina continued to live in the Malcha Mahal, far away from the prying eyes of the Delhi public. Both were known to be as proud and unfriendly as their blue-blooded royal mother. However, thanks to foreign journalists, who managed to befriend the Awadhi siblings, we have glimpses into the lives they led.

For instance, Prince Cyrus apparently ensured that his mother's table setting was always laid out and he refilled her water glass every day. Before long, his sister died too, leaving the prince all alone with his deep sense of injustice for years as well as his complete inability to mingle with commoners. And, bringing the tragic story to a full circle, Prince Cyrus died a recluse himself in November 2017.

What was left of this mysterious royal family was a crumbling and ransacked mahal and stories of their pride, despite them having lived like paupers towards the end of it.

35

Is Bhangarh Fort Really Haunted?

'I think that everybody should go out there and test their curiosity, find a haunted place.'

—Zak Bagans

One of the first names to pop up when talking about haunted places in India is undoubtedly Bhangarh Fort. Sprawling along the foothills of the Aravalli range in Rajasthan, this curious structure was built for Madho Singh I, the brother of Man Singh who was Emperor Akbar's general. Over the years it has gathered a lot of notoriety for being haunted. In fact, the ASI has strictly instructed visitors to keep away from the fort from sunset to sunrise!

So, what is the mystery behind the haunting of Bhangarh Fort? There are mainly two legends associated with this—stories to share with your friends in hushed voices, huddled together on a cold winter's evening.

The Curse of the Shadows

According to the first story, there was a hermit who used to meditate on the hills, close to which the fort was going to be built. Out of respect, permission was requested from the ascetic, whose name was Guru Bala Nath. He gave his go-ahead on the condition that the fort's shadows should never touch his own house, called *Tantric ki Chhatri*, which still overlooks the fort.

This request was honoured by all, until Madho Singh's grandson Ajab Singh added columns to the fort that cast a shadow on Guru Bala Nath's dwellings. That was when his vengeful curse fell on the fort and nearby villages: it would forever remain roofless. As per legend, even today, if anyone tries to build a roof in the village, it mysteriously collapses.

The Tantrik and the Princess

Another legend has it that Ajab Singh had a beautiful stepsister whose name was Ratnavati. The villagers loved this lovely princess as much as they hated her brother, and there was no dearth of marriage proposals for her. Besides her many suitors, there was a black magic practitioner who was wildly in love with her, but knew that he stood no chance.

What he did, thus, was enchant a bottle of perfume her maid was buying at the village one day, when she was out with the princess, shopping. This was to cast a love spell on Ratnavati; however, she realized this and threw the bottle away. The enchanted bottle became a huge boulder, which went rolling and crushed the wizard.

Before dying, he cursed them, the princess's family and the entire village, saying they would never be reborn. Within a year, a terrible war ensued that caused the death of Ratnavati and most of the army. The curse apparently ensured that all the dead in the fort and the village stayed on as ghosts—still haunting the area after centuries.

NIGHTS AT BHANGARH

As mentioned earlier, no visitors are allowed in the fort before daybreak. And those daring souls who have ventured there in the dark have claimed to have experienced unnatural phenomena—sounds of screaming and crying, even music and dance, the clinking of bangles, weird smells as well as strange lights and shadows.

The truth of these can be ascertained only if you are brave enough to go visit it after sundown yourself. Keep in mind that it certainly carries the notoriety of being one of the most haunted places in India, as well as a popular suicide spot.

Paranormal experts who have conducted extensive investigations here have not really discovered anything suspicious, and the vendors

> **THE LESSER-KNOWN GHOST VILLAGE**
>
> If you ever visit Bhangarh, do not forget to also check out Ajabgarh—a neighbouring village just 15 kilometres away, which abounds in similar experiences and stories of evil sorcerers and strange sightings.

in the surroundings of the fort enjoy good business due to rise of interest in this historic monument. However, the eeriness lingers long after common sense has convinced you that Bhangarh Fort may not be all that haunted. It will remain a mystery for years to come.

36

The Mystery Behind the Georgia Guidestones

'We are living on the brink of the apocalypse, but the world is asleep.'

—Joel C. Rosenberg

If the world were to end tomorrow, and you were one of the few people left alive, how would you go about rebuilding your life and human society in general? That's a loaded question that will probably take you more than just a few seconds to figure out. However, there have been huge amounts of literature and philosophy that have already been churned out about life after an apocalypse.

You can find one such tangible answer in Georgia, US. A strange monument that has been the centre of much controversy since its erection 40 years ago in 1980, it is either hailed as the pillar of knowledge for a post-apocalyptic world or as the devil's plan to destroy humanity.

WHAT IS IT?

At first glance, the Georgia Guidestones look like a modern version of the ancient Stonehenge—five tall slabs of granite erected in a circular arrangement, with capstones placed on top of them. It is no wonder the monument is also referred to as the American Stonehenge. Standing tall at over 19 feet, the outer four slabs have 10 guidelines inscribed on them that are the reason behind the popular outcries of devilry and Satanism. The commandments are given in eight languages—English, Russian, traditional Chinese, Arabic, Spanish, Swahili, Hebrew and Hindi.

WHO BUILT IT?

It was a summer day in June 1979, when a mysterious man who called himself Robert C. Christian approached a local construction company to commission the structure. All was well while he briefed the representative about how the structure needed to function as a clock and a calendar, and be sturdy enough to withstand any catastrophic event. It was when he brought up the guidelines to be inscribed on the monument that the builders decided he was a little deranged and tried to dissuade him by quoting an exorbitant cost.

> ### A SECRET NEVER TO BE REVEALED
>
> The anonymous group that funded the monument wanted to keep its identity so secret that they made the builders sign a non-disclosure agreement. After the project was over, they were sworn to destroy all legal documents related to the construction of the Guidestones.

Christian calmly accepted the price, explaining how he and a small anonymous group of loyal Americans had been planning the monument for 20 years. The astrological specifications for the structure were so intricate and complicated that the company had to bring in an astronomer from the University of Georgia to construct it.

Facing backlash from the public even as it was being built, the Georgia Guidestones was finally unveiled in March 1980.

WHAT DOES IT SAY?

'Let these be Guidestones to an Age of Reason.'

With this line, the 10 controversial guidelines begin. The first two talk about keeping the population under 500 million and giving more attention to fitness and diversity over numbers. These were the most debated guidelines, as critics pointed out that the authors sought to wipe out over 95 per cent of the population. However, if seen from a post-apocalyptic perspective, it makes sense that a certain number needs to be maintained without harming nature.

The third asked humanity to unite with one new language. This was deemed as a mark of the Antichrist by Christians quoting the Bible.

The fourth sought to approach everything—including religion and tradition—with reason. This too was taken as an attack on Christianity.

The others pointed towards a fair political, judicial and environmental approach to society.

WHAT DOES IT DO?

Besides bearing guidelines to a utopian society, the structure also spoke of a time capsule buried underneath it. However, the date on which it was to be opened had been left blank, leading people to believe that it was never actually buried. It also told the time of the day and the date, by guiding the rays of the sun through slits in its slabs. The secret group that commissioned it probably wanted it to be a guide in more ways than one, if the planet ever faced a devastating catastrophe that humans needed to recover from.

WHAT DID PEOPLE SAY?

From being called the Ten Commandments of the Antichrist to a monument by a Luciferian secret society, the Georgia Guidestones have garnered as much hatred as awe. The most common conspiracy theory is that the name of the mysterious man Robert C. Christian is a derivation of Christian Rosenkreuz, the founder of the Rosicrucian Order—a society that believed in supposed ancient secrets of different religions across the world kept hidden from the general public that will guide humanity.

Historians have also pointed out that it could have been built as a reaction to the then-ongoing Cold War, which could have precipitated into a World War III, causing humanity to rebuild itself in a post-apocalyptic era.

The secret behind the anonymous group that commissioned the Guidestones has never been revealed. Whether they are a work of a Satanic cult or a mysterious group of intellectuals, one thing is certain: if humanity were to face a devastating blow, these guidelines would be a solid starting point to rebuild a broken world.

37

The Winchester Mystery House

> *'Each person is an enigma. You're a puzzle not only to yourself but also to everyone else, and the great mystery of our time is how we penetrate this puzzle.'*
>
> —Theodore Zeldin

Stairs that take you nowhere. Doors that open up to walls. Windows that open to other rooms. Sounds puzzling? Welcome to the mysterious Winchester House in California, that has captivated the imagination of locals and tourists for almost a century.

THE HISTORY

The Winchester House was built by Sarah Winchester, the widow of a very wealthy firearms mogul. So wealthy, that after he passed away in 1881, Mrs Winchester received what would amount to $532 million in 2018. Besides this, since she received nearly 50 per cent ownership of the Winchester Repeating Arms Company. Her daily income at that time would amount to $26,000 in 2018!

These fortunes of Sarah Winchester are important to note because these are exactly what paid for the intriguing house she continued to build till her death.

THE MYSTERY

Deaths in the family can take you to dark places. When both Sarah's husband as well as her infant daughter passed away one after the other, legend has it that she started consulting a medium. The medium apparently took on the spirit of her deceased spouse and told her that she and her family were haunted and that she must leave her home in New Haven, Connecticut, and travel west. There she was to build a home for the souls of all the people killed by Winchester rifles to appease them.

She followed the advice of her spiritualist, and three years later, was in possession of an incomplete farmhouse in Santa Clara Valley in North California. This became the skeleton structure for Sarah Winchester's maniacal masonry.

THE HOUSE

A house that continued to be a work in progress till her death, it was built to seven storeys, but after an earthquake hit it, it was reduced to four. Built without any consultation from architects, only following Mrs Winchester's whims and fancies, it was as odd as it was grand. Here are some amazing facts about this confounding structure:

- 78,000 litres of paint were needed to paint the entire place.
- It housed 161 rooms: 40 bedrooms, two ballrooms, 47 fireplaces, 17 chimneys, two basements and three elevators.
- The windows and doors used over 10,000 panes of glass. Many of the stained window panes were designed by the famous Tiffany Company, and some by the designer Tiffany himself.
- The chandeliers were gold and silver, the flooring was hand-inlaid parquet and the stairs were crafted to be easily climbed by the steadily arthritic Winchester widow.
- Sarah Winchester was obsessed with the spider-web pattern and the number 13. Both feature in a stained glass designed by her that was never installed but stored in what was called the '$25,000-storage room'. This room apparently was filled with objects that were together worth $25,000, or $374,000 in 2018.

> **PLAYING HIDE-'N'-SEEK WITH SPIRITS**
>
> For a house with so many rooms, it had only one functional toilet. All the others were built as decoys to confuse spirits if they chose to haunt them. This is also the reason why Sarah Winchester slept in a different bedroom every night, and would use secret passageways to go from one room to another.

- The house boasted features rare during its time, such as push-button gas lights, indoor plumbing, a hot shower and indoor heating.

Contractors working at the Winchester House spoke of how Mrs Winchester used to communicate with benevolent spirits daily through her medium, and the direction the construction of the house took depended on what the spirits commanded her to do. And these supernatural diktats ensured that the house was constantly in a state of construction—a window here, a stairway there—a living, breathing structure mutating over the years till Mrs Winchester died in 1922.

No relative has since spoken about the house and the mystery behind it. In fact, Mrs Winchester herself never gave any interviews or left any journals that mention it.

The house has since been cleared of all her possessions, sold off to an investor and continues to be open to the public. Although paranormal investigations have turned up nothing, visitors to the Winchester Mystery House report feeling haunted inside. For a home built to house restless spirits, it would not be out of place to experience such sensations there, would it?

SUPERNATURAL ELEMENTS

38

Salem Witch Trials

'That is the essence of a witchhunt, that any questioning of the evidence or the procedures in itself constitutes proof of complicity.'

—Bergen Evans

Late seventeenth century was a dark time for humanity in colonial Massachusetts, US. The region was reeling from the after-effects of a war with France, a smallpox epidemic, animosity with the nearby Native American tribes as well as the rich community of the neighbouring city of present-day Salem. Amidst these tensions came an event so shocking that it has not only left a bitter taste in the mouth even today, but has also become a historic episode inspiring many works of pop art and culture.

Nineteen people were hanged to death for practising witchcraft in 1692, over a period of four months—and centuries later, that cursed past still haunts the townspeople and descendants of the victims today.

> **THE TOUCH TEST OF WITCHES**
>
> Did you know that the people back then believed that witches passed evil on to innocent victims through tiny particles from their eyes and they could take back the evil by touching the sufferers? This was a test given to the accused, where they had to touch (allegedly) afflicted people. If they stopped screaming, then it apparently proved that the accused did practise witchcraft!

THE MANIFESTATIONS

Who are witches, really? If we travel back in time to a period when the fear of witches—apparently empowered by the devil himself—was at its height among conservative Christians, you will realize that the term 'witch' might as well have been used to define anyone who did not walk the narrow strict path of religion.

It all began when two young girls started experiencing convulsions and bouts of screaming, as well as twisting into scary contortions. When the local doctor could not find a cause behind this, he suspected something supernatural was at hand. The blame went to an old coloured slave Tituba, a homeless beggar Sarah Good, and a poor old lady Sarah Osborn—who the girls accused of bewitching them.

While the latter two denied their charges, Tituba confessed—allegedly because she was beaten into confession and coached into what to say—which she believed would help her escape conviction. It was just the beginning.

By the time it was over, over 200 men and women were accused of witchcraft and interrogated. Fourteen women and five men were hanged, another man crushed to death and more than five people perished in jails.

THE MADNESS

Around 75 per cent of the victims were female. The conservative Christians—called the Puritans—believed that although both men and women were equal in the eyes of God, it was not the same for the devil. He apparently found women's souls unprotected and bodies weak enough to possess them.

Additionally, historians say that women were more likely to confess to witchcraft because most of them truly believe they had been taken by the devil, while others admitted guilt just in the hope of being spared.

The signs of odd behaviour were definitely there—screaming, throwing things, talking in different tongues, crawling under furniture, and more. While these were certainly causes for concern, historians believe they were not always real. Allegations were sometimes made over petty matters such as quarrelling with neighbours.

THE CAUSE

At the time, the strange behaviour of the young women was believed to be of an unholy origin. Later, it was thought to have been caused by hysteria. Almost 300 years later, in 1972, the theory of rye bread poisoning was put forward by scientists. The fungus ergot, found in rye as well as wheat and other cereals, can cause muscle spasms, vomiting, as well as hallucinations. Ergot or Claviceps purpurea is a natural substance from which hallucinogenic drugs such as LSD are derived.

THE PRESENT

The spate of executions, accusations and episodes started dying down in a few months since it began, with the people under arrest released from jail. Some of the persecutors even apologized for their role in the entire event.

The collective guilt of the Salem community as well as the deep resentment of the descendants have since led to the exoneration of the names of the previously convicted and accused. The mystery of this dark chapter in history is not so much as to what happened, but how it could be allowed to happen. It was a proof of how far religious fanaticism and scapegoating could take society.

> **WHEN AGE DOES NOT MATTER**
>
> The youngest person to be accused of witchcraft during the Salem Witch Trials was a four-year-old girl Dorothy Good. Her mother Sarah Good was one of the first to be accused as well. The oldest person to be accused was an 81-year-old farmer Giles Corey, who refused to confess and was tortured to death by having stones put on his chest one by one till he could not bear the crushing weight any more.

39

Are Vampires Real?

'Death is the one predator we can't escape. But vampires have found the loophole so many of us crave. I think that's the allure of vampirism.'

—Sherrilyn Kenyon

Do you think vampires are mythical creatures? Like unicorns or dragons? What if you found out they are very much real and live among us? Are they spooky like in Bram Stoker's *Dracula* or attractive and cool like in Stephenie Meyer's Twilight series?

The mystery of the blood-drinking monsters has lit up the collective imagination of the world for hundreds of years. There are many stories, explanations and myths from different countries that contribute to our understanding of this supernatural figure.

WHAT MAKES A VAMPIRE?

Beliefs about the characteristics that define a vampire differ from place to place, but there are certain common ones.

- They drink human blood for sustenance using their sharp fangs
- They come out to hunt only at night, as sunlight weakens their powers
- They have super strength and a hypnotic effect on victims
- They can transform into bats
- They do not cast reflections or shadows, because they apparently have no soul
- Lastly, they are immortal

FOLK ORIGINS

That said, you will be surprised to know popular idea of pale, beautiful vampires were far from the vampires that people used to hunt down in eighteenth-century Europe. The lack of knowledge was as widespread as contagious illnesses back then. Whenever people used to die from consumption or pulmonary tuberculosis, amongst other diseases, people believed they turned into vampires who would wake up from their coffin and go feeding.

Villagers would dig up the grave of the suspected vampire. This would usually be one who died first, among others, due to a contagious sickness, thus affecting others. Their ignorance about how corpses that are a few days or weeks old look like would make them believe that they truly were blood-sucking vampires.

Why? They would be purplish, swollen and bleeding at the mouth or nose—all signs of a decaying body. Unfortunately, they were taken as indicators of a vampire who has become plump after his nightly feeds!

DIFFERENT COUNTRIES, DIFFERENT MYTHS

The presence of blood-sucking demons has been noted in the oral traditions of most countries and are part of regional legends, the earliest of which are the Persians, with their pottery showing creatures trying to drink blood from men. In India itself, Betal and Pishach bear resemblance to the European vampires. The bird-like strix in Roman mythology, the iron-toothed asanbosam in West Africa and the Jiangshi or Chinese vampires are just a few of such vampire-like legendary creatures.

> **NO VAMPIRES, SAYS MATH**
>
> Legend says that all victims of vampires turn into similar blood-sucking monsters themselves. However, a physics professor in Florida argued that it is mathematically impossible based on geometric progression. According to him, if vampires fed once monthly, then the entire human population would have become vampires in less than three years since the first vampire began feeding.

PROTECTION AND DESTRUCTION

To each place its own, but garlic has been a very common item in warding off vampires in most places. Sacred items such as crucifix, holy water and the rosary also kept them off—as did mirrors.

When it comes to killing vampires, driving a wooden stake through their hearts has long been practised in Europe. Aspen wood was one of the preferred materials to make these stakes, because it is believed that Jesus Christ's cross was made from it.

Besides stakes, there were other practices to prevent suspected vampires from rising—decapitation, placing garlic, lemon or metal items inside the mouth, and lastly, incineration. Well, maybe that's why we do not know of any Hindu vampires!

MODERN-DAY VAMPIRES

To our original question as to whether vampires really exist—among us, today—the answer is both yes and no. Yes, there are a number of people today who have opted for the vampire lifestyle, and practitioners of the sanguine vampirism subculture drink human blood as part of a sacred ritual. No, they do not prey on innocent victims or go biting their necks in dark alleys at night.

The craving to drink blood is called haematomania, and for modern vampires it is apparently not voluntary but something they are born with! The feeding is implemented very professionally—with blood reports and certificates issued to willing 'donors'—and trained professionals carry them out.

Less shocking than these sanguine or blood-drinking vampires are the psychic vampires who suck out spiritual nourishment or

> **MURDEROUS VAMPIRES**
>
> There have been cases when murder victims have been discovered with vampiric rituals having been performed on them, especially by serial killers. This included drinking blood of their victims. Famous among them are the German Peter Kürten, known as the Dusseldorf Vampire, and the American Richard Trenton Chase, known as the Vampire of Sacramento.

pranic energy from others. Nonetheless, they belong to a subculture of this alternative lifestyle that is not very well-known in the mainstream. The spooky stories of vampires from centuries ago are nothing compared to these mysterious present-day vampires, right? But that's a story for another day!

STRANGE OCCURRENCES

40

What Caused the Dancing Plague of 1518?

'Truth is always strange, stranger than fiction.'

—Lord Byron

Dance is perhaps the most beautiful expression of emotions. But what if you couldn't stop dancing? It would certainly give the expression 'dance till you drop' a whole new literal meaning!

But that is exactly what happened one summer 500 years ago in Alsace, France. Around 400 people took to dancing on the streets involuntarily for days, some dropping dead out of sheer exhaustion. A number of them suffered heart attacks and strokes and died as well. This dancing mania went on for a month. And till today, we have no exact clue as to what caused this.

THE FIRST DANCE

It was a normal day in July of 1518 in the city of Strasbourg, when a woman, Mrs Troffea, began dancing on the streets. If it was a strange sight, it became even stranger when she did not stop for days! In a week's time, a dozen more joined her. By the time it was a month, there were hundreds of them—mostly women. Some say that around 15 people would collapse every day, dropping dead like flies.

Given that it was a time of superstitions, one would think that there would be a religious or supernatural cause attached to it. But there were none! Everyone, including noblemen and physicians, were stumped. They arrived at the conclusion that it was a natural disease caused by hot blood. Back then, it was a common practice to bleed patients with this diagnosis, but this time the authorities took a radical decision—they let them continue dancing. In fact, they built dancing areas for them and got musicians to play music, so as to let the victims 'dance it out'.

It was a horrible idea as it only increased the number of people joining in. It was only in September that the plague ended when the dancers were taken away to pray at a shrine on top of a mountain.

THE ROOT CAUSE

What happened in 1518 was not an isolated event. This dancing mania occurred in several places in Europe between the fourteenth and seventeenth centuries. Once, a troupe of 200 people plagued by this illness caused a bridge to collapse by dancing on it!

> **TOXIC TWIRLINGS**
>
> The only antidote for bite victims of tarantulas or scorpions in Italy was to dance back then. This would apparently separate the poison from the blood. A summertime phenomenon, people who were bitten, or believed they were, would suddenly start dancing—apparently under the belief that the music reactivated the residual toxins in their blood.

No one knows what caused this mysterious plague till today. There have been some theories though. The psychoactive ergot fungi that grows on rye and other grains could have been the culprit. It contains the same component that is used in hallucinogenic drugs, and was thought to cause other historic events such as the Salem witch trials. But there are various reasons why this was refuted. The drug would not cause spasms and dancing hallucinations for so many days. In other similar cases of dancing mania, the crops in those regions were different.

Psychological causes have also been put forward. The people of this region suffered great starvation and diseases. The plague could have been a cause of psychosis brought on by stress. It is believed that St Vitus, a Catholic saint who the people worshipped, could curse them with a dancing plague. This must have led to mass hysteria, which sceptics have tried to explain as a religious cult activity. In such cases, people start displaying odd behaviour and this spread very quickly—affecting young women mostly. A neurological disorder called chorea, where sufferers make quick and flitting involuntary movements, has also been suspected.

With the end of the Middle Ages, this bizarre chapter also closed. But one cannot help but be fascinated by this mysterious occurrence—more so, as it defies explanation. What do you think, will any dance party you attend ever live up to this historical event? We think not!

41

What Caused the Tunguska Event?

'Russia is a riddle wrapped in a mystery inside an enigma.'

—Winston Churchill

Extraterrestrial spores that create zombies…
A weapon-testing experiment by scientist Nikola Tesla…
Attack by aliens on spaceships…

What these three things have in common is that they all are plots found across pop culture related to the Tunguska Event—and they continue to grow with time. Literature, video games, movies and TV shows pertaining to the science fiction/fantasy genre are awash with such references to this occurrence that happened more than 111 years ago in a remote corner of Russia.

WHAT WAS IT?

The Tunguska Event, simply put, was an enormous explosion that took place near the Podkamennaya Tunguska river in Russia on 30 June 1908. Why it is so significant is that it is the largest impact event (when astronomical bodies collide) on Earth in recorded history, even though there was no actual impact, and whatever was, burst in the atmosphere itself.

> **CASUALTIES, OR THE LACK OF IT**
>
> Russia is the largest country in the world, and among the top 20 sparsely populated ones. Tunguska was particularly even more sparsely populated, hence there are no known human casualties. However, the explosion flattened 2,000 square kilometres of forests, knocking down 80 million trees, reducing hundreds of deer to mere carcasses, and causing an earthquake measuring not less than 5.0 on the Richter scale.

The size of the astronomical body that caused the explosion is generally considered to have been between 60 and 190 metres, disintegrating 5 to 10 kilometres above the earth's surface. The energy released during the explosion was 3 to 5 megatons of TNT—which equals around 200 times that of the Hiroshima bombing.

WHAT DID IT LOOK LIKE?

It was 7:17 a.m. when a column of bright blue light moved across the sky. Ten minutes later there was a flash and loud sounds such as machine gun shots. After the light and sounds followed shockwaves that knocked people off their feet and destroyed property. Airwaves from the explosion were registered as far as the UK and the US. The list of strange occurrences did not end there.

Apparently, the skies in Europe and Asia were strangely luminescent during the night. A space observatory programme in the US noted the decrease in atmospheric transparency for months later. Eyewitness accounts speak of splitting skies, immense heat, loud, cracking noises and scary tremors. No doubt, to the indigenous tribes residing in the region, this event would have appeared no less than the end of the world.

WHAT DID THE INVESTIGATIONS REVEAL?

As a country with an unstable political situation quickly heading to World War I, it was difficult for scientists to study the area right after the explosion. Conspiracy theorists of the time were quick to point out how this could have been a publicity stunt of the contemporary eccentric physicist Nikola Tesla, who was desperate to get attention and funding for his proposed 'death ray' or wireless electricity transmitter.

Initially though, this news was not even published in Moscow. In fact, the first survey took place 13 years after the event by Russian mineralogist Leonid Kunik, who gathered that it was a meteorite impact—although there were no impact craters found.

The climate in the region was much to blame—with a long, dry winter and a short summer when everything turns into a muddy swamp. Whatever must have dropped from the skies was probably all buried in the mush. Chemical analysis revealed high nickel proportions in microscopic spheres in the soil, which is common in meteorites. If it weren't for Kunik's interest, the event would not have gained more scientific notice for many more years to come.

Today, it has been calculated that asteroids entering the earth's atmosphere and bursting in the air is quite common; however, big ones with energy of 5 kilotons occur once a year. Even rarer, meteoroids the size of the Tunguska explosion occur once in 1,000 years!

ASTEROID OR COMET?

Researchers later posited that it was not a meteor, but a comet that exploded. Comets, unlike meteors and asteroids, are not just made of rock but mostly of ice—which would explain the absence of more alien material on the surface. Also, the glowing skies could thus be explained by the evaporation of the ice and dust of the comet into the upper atmosphere. In fact, it has been suggested that the body was a part of a periodic comet, Comet Encke, which causes annual meteor showers towards the end of June.

> **THE MYSTERY LAKE**
>
> Lake Cheko, 8 kilometres from the explosion centre, was identified in 2007 as a possible impact crater. The conical shape of the lake bed pointed towards it being a likely candidate for about a decade until 2017, when Russian soil research proved that it was older than the event, having been there for 280 years or more.

There have been many supporters as well as critics of this theory. While most of the latter have stuck to the asteroid theory, there are others with various other hypotheses. Of these, the most significant one states that it was the release and explosion of 10 million tons of natural gas from inside the Earth's crust, also called a Verneshot. Another theory posits that a small black hole collided with Earth, causing the explosion.

In fact, there are suggestions that it was an alien spaceship that was on its way to Lake Baikal in search of freshwater.

Today, there are over 1,000 scholarly papers on the Tunguska

Event, and counting. Even though it is not the only explosion event that has captured the attention of the world, it is certainly one that has made the maximum impact in our collective minds throughout history.

42

What Happened to the Lost Colony of Ronoake?

'There are plenty of people on Earth. It's not like the human race is going to disappear if a few people don't come back. Exploration is dangerous.'

—William Stone

Do you agree though? Exploration is essential to humans—for survival, for enlightenment, for evolution. But yes, it comes with the caveat that a few brave souls will be sacrificed or go missing in this noble pursuit. What about an entire colony?

THE BACKGROUND

Let's go back to America in the sixteenth century—when the US was still not formed and the first English settlers were still coming in. It was in August 1587 when one such group of 115 emigrants from England arrived and set up their colony at Ronoake Island, close to what we today know as North Carolina. Interestingly, this was not the first attempt, as another party had arrived two years earlier to the island but were not successful in setting up a colony. This was caused by lack of supplies as well as troubles with the nearby Native American tribes.

All was well, till the newly appointed governor of the new settlers' colony, John White, decided to sail back to England for fresh supplies and commodities later that year.

THE INCIDENT

Things started going wrong for these people then on. A major war broke out between England and Spain, causing all English ships to be taken away for battle. White couldn't get back to Ronoake until August of 1590—excited at the prospect of finally returning to his wife, daughter and granddaughter. Shockingly enough for him, the colony and all its inhabitants had completely disappeared. There was no sign or clue—except a wooden post that had the word 'Croatoan' carved on it. It was both the name of a nearby island as well as the Native American tribe living on it.

> **THE FIRST IMMIGRANT BABY IN AMERICA**
>
> One of the first English colonies to settle in America, the Ronoake Colony is also significant for the first English child born in America. Her name was Virginia Dare, John White's own granddaughter.

Ronoake was abandoned, the houses dismantled, anything that could be carried was removed, and White's own trunks had been dug up and looted.

Given the etched word, White surmised that it meant the settlers had relocated to the Croatoan island, but before he could go there to investigate, he had to return to England due to inclement weather at the seas.

THE EXPLANATIONS

It's been over 400 years now, and there have been explanations galore that seek to demystify the occurrence. However, none of them have been close to being satisfactory, purely because of the lack of evidence. Some of the theories are:

- The settlers were murdered or kidnapped by the Native American tribe
- They willingly moved to the mainland and settled there amidst other English immigrants
- They probably tried to sail back to England and got lost at sea
- They were attacked by Spaniards passing through

TODAY

There is still no answer to this Middle Age mystery from America. DNA tests have been initiated to see if the present locals living on the island are related to the early Ronoake settlers or Native American tribes—maybe both. Today, the 115 vanished English people are called the Lost Colony. How could over a hundred people just disappear without any word—except Croatoan? Their contribution as pioneers in the history of America is widely acknowledged today, even though they themselves have vanished into history.

43

What Happened to the *Mary Celeste*?

> 'There is no greater unknown than the sea and no greater mystery than a lost ship.'
>
> —Clive Cussler

An even greater mystery is an abandoned ship in the middle of the ocean with a missing crew. Presenting the *Mary Celeste*, the biggest mystery from the history of the high seas. Often referred to as a cursed ship, there have been innumerable retellings, legends and creative adaptations about this mystifying sailing vessel for more than a century now.

THE OCCURRENCE

On 4 December 1872, a Canadian ship *Dei Gratia* found a mysterious sea vessel moving unsteadily towards it when it was making its way across the Atlantic Ocean. When it reached a little closer, the captain of *Dei Gratia*, David Morehouse, recognized it as the *Mary Celeste* and started sending radio signals to it. There was no answer, and no one seemed to be on the deck. He sent his first and second mate there on a boat to investigate. On boarding the *Mary Celeste*, they found it eerily empty.

Some sails were missing and the rest were found in poor condition. The ropes were damaged, hanging loosely over the sides of the ship. Two hatches leading down to the cargo were opened, but the cargo—alcohol for industrial purposes—was intact. The lifeboat was missing. The binnacle or the stand carrying the ship's navigational instruments was moved and the glass case on it was shattered. There was some water in the lower part of the ship. Nothing belonging to the crew was missing, except the ship's papers and the captain's navigational instruments. There were no signs of any violence.

Most interestingly, the last record noted in the ship's diary or log was dated to nine days back when it was apparently 900 nautical miles from where it was found! What happened to the captain, his family and his crew? What happened for them to either abandon the ship or go missing in the middle of the ocean?

It was brought back to land by the crew of the *Dei Gratia* and examined by professionals. But nothing concrete came to light, although there were multiple theories both during and after the investigations.

THE EXPLANATIONS

Foul Play

Since there was a salvage award paid to the ship that brought back such vessels from the sea, it was suspected that either the *Dei Gratia* captain and crew killed the men on *Mary Celeste* to claim the reward, or that the captains of both ships had planned this to divide the insurance money among themselves. The examination of the ship was conducted under such biased views, wherein evidences of violence and blood were put forward. All such claims were later proven untrue.

> **POISONOUS FUMES**
>
> The cargo contained 1,701 barrels of denatured alcohol—a poisonous substance. Some say that its fumes affected the crew and caused some incidents that led to the ship's abandonment.

Other theories include the crew of *Mary Celeste* killing their captain and escaping an attack by African pirates, who were active in that sea route. Since no valuables were stolen, it has been rejected. Another theory was that the captain, Benjamin Briggs, a devout Christian, killed his crew in a fit of religious mania. This theory too has been withdrawn.

Faulty Instruments

Another explanation put forward is that the instruments of the ship were probably malfunctioning, leading the captain and the crew to believe that the ship was flooding and that they were closer to land than they actually were. This could be the reason they might have escaped on the lifeboat. However, being the experienced seafarer that the captain of the *Mary Celeste* was, it was difficult for most to believe that this could have been the reason.

Natural Phenomenon

From seaquakes (quakes under the sea that cause disturbances on the surface), waterspouts (tornadoes in the ocean), collision with some iceberg, to even an attack by a giant squid—there have been multiple assumptions about what really could have happened to the unlucky *Mary Celeste*. Since there was no actual evidence to back any of them, they did not find support.

Paranormal Intervention

With no actual scientific solution to the intriguing mystery, it is no wonder there have been a number of theories that involve some form of alien activity in the midst of the ocean on the ship, miles away from land. But how does one go about proving it?

THE SHIP

Mary Celeste seemed to have been cursed right from the beginning. The first captain of the ship, Robert McLellan, fell ill during a stop and the ship had to turn back. McLellan died the same month. The ship continued to bring suffering to later captains in its further voyages—colliding with other vessels and sinking them. In 1867, it was wrecked in a storm and so badly damaged that it was abandoned by its captain.

> **THE ORIGIN OF THE NAME**
>
> It is said that the ship was renamed from *Amazon* to *Mary Celeste* after Galileo's illegitimate daughter Marie Celeste.

After it was recovered, resold and restored, it kept on bringing misfortune to all associated with it. In 1879, the then captain of the *Mary Celeste* also fell ill and died prematurely—the third person to do so after McLellan and Briggs.

The end of the ship came when its final owner, with two others, deliberately wrecked the ship to collect insurance. His crimes were discovered and he died of poverty three months later. Of the others, one went mad and the other committed suicide. Even to the most cynical, it seemed that the cursed ship avenged her destruction.

THE LEGENDS

After the ship came under the limelight since its abandonment, there were a lot of misreporting and dubious first-person accounts of people claiming to be associated with the ship and its crew, which added to the apparent myth of the cursed ship. Even in literature, the fictional story written by Arthur Conan Doyle in 1884, then a ship surgeon, titled *J. Habakuk Jephson's Statement*, was almost believed to be the true account of what happened to the *Mary Celeste*.

THE LEGACY

The amount of art, literature and documentaries this ship has inspired is impressive. From radio plays to novels to movies, the *Mary Celeste* has become the epitome of maritime mysteries. However, she is not the only one with such a bewildering incident. In 1955, a ship *MV Joyita* also disappeared in the South Pacific Ocean with 25 people on board. The ship was found a month later, but the people on it were never heard of again.

Disappearances in themselves are a curious event, but for them to happen in the middle of the vast ocean is frightening. Especially when the mystery continues to remain unsolved even after almost 150 years.

44

What Happened to the SS *Ourang Medan*?

'...we float. All officers, including the Captain, dead in chartroom and on the bridge. Probably whole of crew dead...'

—SOS from *Ourang Medan*

THE INCIDENT

This call for help was sent out from the Dutch cargo ship in 1947 (dates differ between sources) and answered by an American merchant ship *Silver Star* navigating the Straits of Malacca 19 hours away. When the *Silver Star* arrived, the *Ourang Medan* was floating 50 miles away from its original location and seemed to be in a normal condition from outside. However, no one from the ship answered to the American ship's messages—which is when their crew climbed on board.

The captain and crew of *Ourang Medan*—22 in total, as well as the ship's dog—were all found dead, their bodies lying all over the ship, their faces frozen with terror and shock. There was no sign of struggle or damage—just a chilling sight of death with no apparent cause. Interestingly, there was one lifeboat missing, which meant that some crew members might have been able to escape whatever caused the tragic incident.

The temperature in the ship was nothing like the warm ocean air that day. In fact, it was chilly. Even without any apparent signs of injury, the bodies seemed to be decomposing at a faster-than-usual rate. The crew of the *Silver Star* decided to tow the boat to the closest harbour. However, they soon noticed that a hold of the ship was emitting strange smoke.

They had just managed to evacuate to their own vessel and detach themselves from the *Ourang Medan* when it apparently exploded and then sank to oblivion.

THE CAUSE

Over the years, many have given their versions of what could have caused this strange phenomenon. From aliens to paranormal activity, there have been many theories associated with this mystery. However, the most likely cause is that the ship was carrying thousands of boxes of illegal toxic substances which might have leaked and caused the deaths. This was, in fact, ratified by a survivor of the ship, who claimed he had deserted the boat with some other crew members (on that missing lifeboat mentioned earlier) when he found out that it was dangerous to be on it.

> ### DOCTOR DOCTOR!
> Interestingly, there are some accounts of the mystery of the SS *Ourang Medan* which says that the SOS that went out on 27 June 1947 was a message asking for a doctor to come onboard. This was before the final spine-chilling SOS about the death of the crew members went out. One wonders if anything could have prevented the tragedy then, or if it was already too late.

THE ACTUAL MYSTERY

While the incident itself seems mysterious and scary, the biggest mystery is the time during which it occurred and the question whether all parts of the story are true. Researchers have found mention of the *Ourang Medan*'s incident in newspaper archives that date back to November 1939—which is way before the *Silver Star* was even constructed.

Nobody knows what the ship even looked like—and there is no record of the *Ourang Medan*'s existence. Since it was around the time of World War II—decades after the Geneva Convention outlawed all chemical weapons—it must not have been a registered ship, if it was truly carrying contraband substances on board.

The same incident was reported in papers in 1940, 1947 and 1948. The account of the survivor—who was the ship's second mate—

was told to a missionary. He passed it on to an Italian author who produced a report on it. The accounts from all different years include this confession to the missionary. Unfortunately, the surviving crew member died a few days after reaching land.

So, did this incident truly happen? If it did, when? And where? Accounts of its location have also varied over time.

The mystery of the SS *Ourang Medan* ship continues to be one of the biggest mysteries from the sea in world history. In fact, it has been told and retold so many times by different sources, that the line between truth and fiction has blurred—leading it to gain the status of a legend today.

45

Who Committed the Nepalese Royal Massacre?

'There are four kinds of homicide: felonious, excusable, justifiable and praiseworthy.'

—Ambrose Bierce

How one would describe the massacre of the Nepalese royal family differs from person to person. It was one of the bloodiest and most infamous familicide (killing of multiple family members) of the twenty-first century. Ten members were killed. Twenty years later, it continues to be steeped in the wildest conspiracies, as the official report is rejected by a majority of the Nepalese public as well as others.

To unravel what probably is one of the most recent mysteries of history, let's travel back to the evening of 1 June 2001 to Tribhuwan Sadan, located in the residence grounds of the Nepalese monarchy.

WHAT REALLY HAPPENED?

It seemed like a regular monthly family reunion dinner for the Nepalese monarchy at their home, the Narayanhity Royal Palace. Siblings, cousins, spouses and children of the extended royal family had all gathered for the occasion. But beneath the apparent calm, something sinister was

> **KATTO: THE SCAPEGOAT RITUAL**
>
> On the eleventh day of the king's death, a vegetarian Brahmin is made to eat non-vegetarian food, dress in the king's clothes and then made to leave the kingdom on the back of an elephant. The Nepalese believe that by doing so, all the bad karma of the dead king will be absorbed by the scapegoat. It is believed by many that the meal contains body parts of the deceased king!

lurking. It wasn't long before gunfire broke out, killing King Birendra, Queen Aishwarya, their children Prince Niranjan and Princess Shruti and five more people, while injuring four others. Eyewitnesses say it was Crown Prince Dipendra who opened fire and later shot himself.

Dipendra was comatose for three days, declared king in that condition, finally dying on 4 June. After his death, the dead king Birendra's brother Gyanendra was made king.

WHO REALLY DID IT?

Interestingly, the Nepalese authorities have not officially revealed the perpetrator, although eyewitnesses and the inquiry reports say it was Crown Prince Dipendra. Having said that, there are multiple theories about the 'actual' culprit.

Prince Dipendra

Apparently, the king-to-be was involved in a romantic relationship with Devyani Rana, the daughter of a rival royal family. His family, especially his mother, refused them permission to get married, which is said to have driven Dipendra to fury. Thus he turned violent that fateful night and then attempted suicide. However, critics disagree. Firstly, he was right-handed, but the self-inflicted wound that later killed him was on the left temple. And there were two bullets, not one! Secondly, the apparent lack of security at such a gathering was suspicious. Why were there no bodyguards to stop the massacre? Thirdly, it was a two-week investigation without major forensic analysis. In fact, the offer by Scotland Yard to investigate the incident was declined.

> **THE INDIAN CONNECTION**
>
> The mother of Dipendra's love interest Devyani is the daughter of Usha Raje Scindia—the Rajmata of Gwalior—and the sister of Vasundhara Raje, the former chief minister of Rajasthan. What is interesting is that Dipendra's mother did not want him to marry Devyani because she believed that the royal family of Gwalior was beneath them!

King Gyanendra

Suspiciously enough, the dead king Birendra's brother was missing from the party. None of his immediate family members who were present were killed. Besides, he and his son Paras were very unpopular with the public. He also destroyed the building where the massacre occurred, raising further misgivings among critics. Although he could not have committed the crime himself, it is alleged that he might have conspired with others to execute his best-laid plans to claim the throne.

RAW

One of the co-conspirators is allegedly the Indian Intelligence agency Research and Analysis Wing. India and Nepal had slight tensions regarding border activity and other sensitive topics and it is believed that they carried out a planned attack.

CIA

Yes, it does go deeper. There are many who believe another co-conspirator was the American Central Intelligence Agency. It is difficult to prove any of this, but online forums are full of theories about how a team of 10 Navy Seals arrived a month before the incident specifically to help carry it out.

Nepal Army

Gyanendra, RAW and the CIA together could not have carried out such an elaborate plan without any inside help. Hence, conspiracy theorists believe that even the Nepal Army had a hand in executing this bloody carnage.

MORE THEORIES, MORE CONSPIRACIES

There are other candidates as well. While some believe that it was Paras, Gyanendra's son, who caused it, others believe China might very well have had a hand as well. Many questions still hover over the shocking incident. Even if the RAW, the CIA and the Nepal Army were involved in this, how has it been possible to keep the truth from coming out for so long?

There are even theories that Dipendra did not kill himself but was shot by someone else! Close acquaintances of the Crown Prince have even claimed that he would have easily given up the throne, but was not someone who could commit such a heinous crime.

It's been two decades since the Narayanhity Palace was splattered with the blood of its royalty. Ask any Nepali and chances are, they would still be doubtful of the report suggesting Dipendra is responsible for the massacre. People continue to demand a fair probe into this mysterious event that rocked Nepal. And thus, question marks continue to hover over the bloody pages of this country's history.

UNKNOWN ENTITIES

46

Who Were the Nine Unknown Men?

'Knowledge is a weapon. I intend to be formidably armed.'

—Terry Goodkind

They say a little knowledge is a dangerous thing. But what is even more dangerous is if the said knowledge falls in the wrong hands and is misused. Enter the Nine Unknown Men, a secret society formed during King Ashoka's rule, who were apparently given the responsibility of keeping secret immense knowledge in key scientific and other areas.

You must have heard of the Illuminati and other secret societies, but this one here is so old and legendary that it is a mystery whether it truly existed or not. Let's investigate!

THE BIRTH

School history lessons on the Kalinga War will tell you how Emperor Ashoka was disillusioned with war after the killing of around a lakh warriors during the war. That was when he converted to Buddhism and became instrumental in the spread of the religion to different parts of Asia. The other significant outcome of his transformation was to try and curb violence and destruction at any cost.

And as legend goes, this is how the Nine Unknown Men were formed. Ashoka brought together nine of the most brilliant minds of his kingdom to form a secret society. He tasked them with the study

> **NINE GEMS OF INDIAN KINGS**
>
> It was a common feature in the courts of the kings of India to have a group of nine extraordinarily gifted men, who were called 'Navratnas' or 'Nine Gems'. King Vikramaditya, the Mughal emperor Akbar and Bengal's ruler Raja Krishnachandra all had their not-so-secret club of nine gifted men.

and collection of scientific knowledge which, in the wrong hands, could have been used for warfare and destruction. All of this knowledge was divided into nine subjects and collated in nine books—with each member in charge of one book.

THE BOOKS

So, what were these secret books about? There are various theories, but the generally accepted list of nine books was the one put forward in 1923 by English-American writer Talbot Mundy.

These books contained subjects ranging from the art of warfare, the 'touch of death' or how to kill a person by a simple touch that reverses nerve impulse, knowledge of the cholera vaccine, a study of metals and extraterrestrial life to the science of gravitation, building airships and time travel.

THE CONTINUANCE

If you thought that the Nine Unknown Men belonged to the past, you are wrong. Legend has it that although they kept their identity undisclosed, they would reveal themselves to their successors so that the secret knowledge could be passed on from one generation to the next. And thus, first formed in 270 BC, this secret society has apparently continued to exist for more than 2,000 years!

Over time, foreigners such as Pope Sylvester II, French writer Jacolliot and bacteriologist Alexandre Yersin, among others, are said to have come in contact with the Nine Unknown Men and benefited greatly.

CONNECTED LEGENDS

It is said that Emperor Ashoka, besides charging the nine men to gather and keep secret the knowledge of these various sciences and arts, also asked them to mould the image of India in the eyes of the world in such a way that it seemed to be a land of mysticism and ignorance. This was supposed to safeguard the actual truth of the immense knowledge that they had in their hands.

Another legend goes that Emperor Ashoka formed the group and safeguarded these advanced scientific technologies so as to preserve the ancient Rama Empire. However, according to Hindu scriptures, this empire was destroyed more than 15,000 years ago by highly advanced weaponry.

It has also been put forward that the Rama Empire and the kingdom of Atlantis got into nuclear warfare, destroying both civilizations and thus raising the need to keep the knowledge of such advanced technologies secret. While this might be a little too far-fetched to believe, the belief in this secret society is not a thing of the past.

THE MEN TODAY

Believers in this secret society say that these men are very much real and continue to work for the betterment of the world. In fact, the nine books are being rewritten continuously over time—the knowledge contained in which can potentially be very hazardous to humanity if it reaches the wrong hands.

Is it real? On the one hand, there is no smoke without fire. On the other, it might very well be all smokes and mirrors. This mystery of history is one we cannot solve without seeing actual evidence—which seem to not be there, or maintained too secretly to be believable!

> **WAS J.C. BOSE ONE OF THEM?**
>
> It is believed that Jagdish Chandra Bose, who pioneered radio and microwave optics, was one of the members of the Nine Unknown Men. Another suspected member was Vikram Sarabhai who contributed immensely to Indian space and missile defence programmes.

47

Who Was Jack the Ripper?

'My knife's so nice and sharp I want to get to work right away if I get a chance.'

—Jack the Ripper

One of the most fascinating, and equally gruesome, topics you will come across when studying history is crime—specifically serial killers. This is so because not only do they tell of the horrible acts a human being is capable of, but also offer an insight into the psychology of a criminal mind. And few serial killers are as famous as Jack the Ripper. This dreaded killer from nineteenth-century England still remains a hot topic of discussion among crime enthusiasts as well as historians.

> **ORIGINAL PSEUDONYMS**
>
> Jack the Ripper was previously called 'The Whitechapel Murderer' or 'Leather Apron'. The name stuck after one of his supposed letters was found to be signed 'Jack the Ripper'.

WHY?

Because even after a series of murders and a huge number of suspects, his identity continues to remain a mystery.

Because he didn't just kill his victims, he punished their bodies in unimaginable ways.

Because he was either so sly or crazy (or both) that he allegedly even wrote letters about his murders and sent them to the police!

THE BACKGROUND

The year was 1888. The place was Whitechapel, London. While this capital city of England thrived and the rich class lived a grand life, the poorer districts painted a sadder picture. One of these districts was Whitechapel, which was mired in poverty and crime. While theft and murder were common here, a series of brutal murders in and around this slum area shook up the entire country. All the murder victims of Jack the Ripper were found to be women.

STYLE OF MURDER

Policemen and detectives came to identify whether a murder was committed by Jack by studying the way the victim was killed. In a number of victims, some organs were found to be missing. Investigators found that the wounds and injuries became progressively worse with each new prey.

THE ACTUAL CRIMES

Till date, there are debates about how many of these murders were actually committed by him. However, there were five that most experts agree were the handiwork of this unknown killer. Those five victims are today known as the Canonical Five, murdered between 31 August and 9 November of 1988.

But there were two more murders before the Canonical Five, and others later—together called the Whitechapel Murders, that could possibly have been the work of Jack the Ripper. Forensic experts deny it because the method of killing were not exactly the same for them, even though they were pretty similar.

RIPPER'S LETTERS

Imagine a murderer writing to the police and giving them hints about a crime he is about to commit or giving evidence that he is the perpetrator of a murder already discovered? Sounds almost like a movie, doesn't it? But history is a script only in retrospect.

At the time of the murders, there were hundreds of letters being sent to the police about the crimes—some to aid with the investigation, and a rare few claiming to have been written by the murderer himself. While most of them turned out to be hoaxes, there were three in particular that were considered important to the Jack the Ripper legacy.

The first one said how the next victim's ears would be cut off—and three days later, that's exactly what happened with one Catherine Eddows. The second one spoke of a double murder. The third one actually arrived with a box containing half a kidney of a supposed victim preserved in ethanol.

However, the police later claimed that the letters were sent by a local journalist who wanted to add more sensationalism to the incidents and sell more copies of the newspaper he worked for. Even though the letters still exist, they have been handled by too many people by now to be able to provide any forensic evidence, shrouding yet another element of this curious case into further mystery.

SUSPECTS

For a crime of this magnitude, you would think that the police would have had some suspects and made some arrests. And you are not wrong. They conducted interviews with over 2,000 people, from whom more than 300 were closely investigated, and around 80 people were detained. Eyewitnesses have reported seeing the victim last with a certain man, but the description of the man was never uniform.

> **LITERARY SUSPECTS**
>
> Lewis Carroll, author of *Alice's Adventures in Wonderland*, was also one of the suspects!

Interestingly, because of the way the crimes were committed, the most common suspects were butchers and surgeons. Over 100 suspects were named in the entire series of investigations, but none was convincing enough. From immigrants such as Polish Jews to Russians, and from mental patients to revengeful husbands and lovers, history is littered with people named as suspects. And not all of them were men either.

Even Sir Arthur Conan Doyle, the creator of the popular detective series Sherlock Holmes, has forwarded a theory about 'Jill the Ripper'. According to this, the killer was probably a midwife—which meant that bloodstains on her clothes would not seem suspicious.

Or was Jack the Ripper more than one person? There have been theories about that as well.

POPULAR CULTURE

The number of books and movies about this legendary killer are many. The term 'Ripperology' has been coined for the sole purpose of defining the study and investigations into his identity and crimes. If that were not enough to fill the curiosity of people, there are even guided tours of the murder sites, and there is now a Jack the Ripper Museum in East London!

Who was this mad killer who roamed the streets of London at night? In 2006, he was voted as the 'worst Briton in history', even though we still do not know who he really was. And after more than a hundred years of the best minds in the world investigating it, the verdict is: we probably shall never truly know.

48

Who Was Lucy the Australopithecus?

*'Evolution is the fundamental idea in all of
life science—in all of biology.'*

—Bill Nye

What is your favourite subject in science? Chemistry, physics or biology? If it is the last, we can assure you there is no topic as fascinating as evolution. It took millions of years for *Homo sapiens* to evolve from their ancestors to become the upright-walking, non-arboreal creatures that have gone on to become the most intelligent species on Earth!

And Lucy the Australopithecus is an intriguing link in the middle of this development that gives us a direct insight into the process of evolution.

> **THE SECRET BEHIND THE NAME 'LUCY'**
>
> The evening after the discovery of the bones, the song 'Lucy in the Sky with Diamonds' by The Beatles played on loop at the expedition camp where all the scientists were staying. The name stuck and the bag of bones became a human entity in the minds of everyone—Lucy.

WHO IS LUCY?

Without creating further suspense, let me reveal to you that Lucy is nothing but a collection of bones discovered by a group of scientists in 1974 in Ethiopia. What is astonishing about this discovery is that 40 per cent of the bones were recovered strewn across the site—and these have helped scientists put together the skeleton of a young female adult from 3.2 million years ago, belonging to the hominin species

Australopithecus afarensis, now extinct. Thus she was older than the other hominin fossils found at that time.

THE DISCOVERY

Lucy's discovery was by pure chance, as the scientists had already scoured the area before without finding anything. However, her being found was fated, because one of the researchers went back on a hunch and first found an arm bone, then a small fragment of the skull, and then, with the entire team, all the bones in the next three weeks. Imagine a human jigsaw puzzle, being put together bit by bit, bringing alive its history. Even though all its bones were not found, the findings were significant to change our understanding of evolution.

It is not every day that scientists make such a historical discovery—and Lucy soon became a household name and she was exhibited across the US for six years. In the Amharic language of Ethiopia, she is known as Dinkinesh, meaning 'you are marvellous'. Well, marvellous she is—seeing how her bones gave the scientists clear ideas about how this species used to live millions of years ago.

THE FINDINGS

First catalogued as AL 288-1, the bone fragments were personified as Lucy by the team. After reconstruction, she stood at 3 feet 7 inches and must have weighed 29 kilograms. She looked somewhat like a chimpanzee, with the animal's small brain.

Lived on Both Trees and Land

As an Australopithecus, Lucy was part of a transitional species, carrying traits that were similar to both earlier apes as well as later *Homo sapiens*. Her long arms suggested that she used to climb trees, like her ancestors. But her pelvis and leg bones are almost similar to modern-day humans, which means that she could stand upright and walk erect.

Bipedal First, Then Big-Brained

Earlier, it was believed that hominins—or a family including humans and primates, except the gorilla genus—first developed big brains and then the skill for walking erect. However, this changed with the discovery of Lucy, whose bones clearly showed walking skills, but a brain one-third of that of humans.

Death Theories

Some scientists argue that Lucy's bone fragments can prove that she probably died by falling down from a tree, although others are not quite convinced. In any case, she is believed to have been 12 years of age at the time of her death.

THE POSSIBILITIES

Even though the Australopithecus genus is extinct, it is believed that one of its species launched the Homo genus, which ultimately went on to make us *Homo sapiens*. Interestingly, we still do not know who the direct ancestor of the Home sapien is! Since the Australopithecus afarensis died out roughly 2.8 million years ago, about the same time that our genus arose, it is not difficult to suppose that Lucy could very well have been our ancestor.

She is not as much a mystery as a key to the mystery of evolution of the human species. Lucy today rests where she was found—at her homeland, Ethiopia, to avoid constant movement which will cause damage to these unique fossils. But casts of her bones have been used to reconstruct her skeleton for display at American museums.

49

Who Were the Vikings?

'Because the Vikings never documented anything—they couldn't read or write—the history is always gonna be a little up in the air.'

—Travis Fimmel

What comes to your mind when you hear the word Vikings? The television series? Movies such as *Thor* or *How to Train Your Dragon*? What about comic series such as *Asterix*? Or maybe something else? No matter what, Vikings bring to mind strappy brutal warriors with battle gear and axes and horned helmets—either fighting wars or feasting loudly with chunks of meat and mugs of ale.

When it comes to these famed Europeans, popular culture is awash with stories and representations—not all of which are correct. Since the Vikings did not read or write themselves, all we have are descriptions about them recorded by other communities and groups—not all of which are unbiased. So, who were the real Vikings? Let's look into this mystery.

SEAFARERS, BUSINESSMEN, WARRIORS

For those who have never been introduced to the Vikings, they were a European community that thrived between the eighth and ninth centuries, mainly in Denmark, Norway and Sweden. This came to be known as the Viking Age—a period when these people plundered as well as carried out business, not only across their homelands in Northern Europe, but beyond as well.

They were excellent sailors and their explorations took them to places far and wide across the world. These travels and trade—and of course raids—became a significant element in the histories of all these places. Coming from the cold Northern European climes, the goods that these Norsemen traded were mostly furs, tusks, seal fat used to seal boats, and slaves.

THE BEGINNING OF THE END

Once Christianity began making inroads into the Scandinavian region, the Viking Age slowly died out. Rulers began to be legitimized by the Catholic Church and the economies began to be modelled after England and Germany. Slavery ended and so did much of their trading by the Vikings. Most of the erstwhile Vikings were now participating in the Crusades of the twelfth and thirteenth centuries.

> **WATERY GRAVES OF THE VIKINGS**
>
> Did you know that the Vikings followed what is called 'ship burial'? They put their dead on a ship or a boat, sometimes loaded it with items (which sometimes included the sacrificed slaves of the dead!) to be sent to the other world and let it float in the water! Even for the ones who were buried on land, 'stone ships' were used. This meant that the burial ground was outlined by slabs of stones set into the ground in the shape of a ship.

THE MYTHS

We have been so bombarded with Viking stereotypes, we never questioned their legitimacy. The best way to understand the Vikings is by tearing away at the myths that have built up around their identity.

Myth #1: Personal Upkeep Was Not a Priority

To us, Vikings bring to mind men with long, bushy, tangled hair and beards. On the contrary, they used tweezers, razors and combs as part of their regular beauty regime. Clearly they took great care of their appearance. They did not live in dirty shacks, but in homes with bright, beautiful halls to throw lavish parties in.

Myth #2: Illiteracy and Barbarianism Was a Way of Life

This was a myth propagated by the Christian writers who looked down upon the Vikings as ignorant brutes. While Vikings did not have a practice of reading and writing, they did have their own system of symbols called the runes. These runes were etched on stones to mark significant events like expeditions and deaths and commemorating brave Vikings. Even without a written legacy, they have been known to be some of the most intelligent naval engineers famous for the Viking long ship that crossed the difficult North Atlantic Ocean with ease.

Myth #3: They Were Godless Heathens

This was another myth by the Christian scribes. The religious beliefs of the Vikings were passed down through oral tradition—a rich tapestry of cosmology and ceremonies. Unlike popular religious groups that gathered in different forms of temples, the Vikings—just like the ancient Celts—used to practise their faith in natural settings such as groves and by the river.

Myth #4: They Were Vicious and Cruel

This was a period of time when violence was the order of the day, and while Viking raiders do fit the bill, it is incorrect to paint the entire community with the same brush. Most of them were seafaring traders who lived peacefully. Besides, there were other kings during that time such as King Charlemagne. He was himself a violent king who carried out genocides. However, in the books of Christian historians, this did not count as a crime as the ones being killed by him were pagans.

> **STRIKING VIKING MUSIC**
>
> Love heavy metal music? Curious about Viking mythology? Combine both and what you have is Viking metal—a niche sub-genre that emerged from black metal in the 1980s. Not a metal fan? Not a problem. You can try some Viking rock, but beware! This genre is highly controversial for being essentially racist.

Myth #5: Women Were Ill-Treated

On the contrary! Viking women had property rights far ahead of most communities of their time. They were leaders of clans in the absence of suitable men. They were allowed to divorce their husbands, be in open relationships and practise all professions—they were warriors, priestesses, merchants and rune masters.

Myth #6: Horned Helmets Were Part of Their Attire

The most important myth to be busted—made necessary by representations in popular media—is this! Can you imagine the awkwardness in battling with axes and hammers—studded helmets that would cause more inconvenience than help? One would be in fear of harming one's own side by wearing such gear. Nowhere in history has Viking horned helmets been mentioned. The only use for horns they had was for drinking. And no, they did not use skulls to drink out of either. That's another myth that needed busting!

50

Who Was the Zodiac Killer?

*'The police shall never catch me, because
I have been too clever for them.'*

—the Zodiac Killer

He was right. This serial killer from California managed to stay anonymous—and not for a dearth of suspects! Murders. Cryptograms. Paranoia. The pure sensationalism around the string of killings has inspired a whole lot of books, movies, music and video games. And why shouldn't it? This killer was as sneaky as attention-seeking, playing hide-and-seek with the police and the media for a decade through intimidating letters and cryptic puzzles.

This is the story of the Zodiac Killer—a mysterious murderer from the US around half a century ago.

VICTIMS

The Zodiac Killer, or Zodiac—as he liked to call himself—claimed to have killed 37 people. However, as far as the victim count goes, investigators have confirmed only five victims who died and two who survived.

- The first of these—called the Lake Herman Road attack—was in December 1968. A couple hanging out in their car were shot by the Zodiac who pulled up next to them in a car.
- The second one in July 1969 also involved a couple in a car. This time the male victim, Michael Mageau, survived, even though Zodiac returned to shoot both of them twice after already firing at them five times. He heard Mageau moaning. Guess what he did next? He went to the nearest phone booth

and made a call to the local police department announcing the murder, and left!
- Again, in September 1969, the couple he attacked were picnicking on a small island at Lake Berrysea. Instead of using his gun, he tied his victims up with rope and stabbed them repeatedly. This time, before calling the police, he first left the record of his murder written on the car of the male victim (who also survived), along with a symbol that went on to become synonymous with the Zodiac. It was a cross symbol over a circle that resembled a target.
- The fifth confirmed victim was one Paul Stine in October 1969, whose cab the Zodiac boarded and then shot him in the head. The serial killer tore off a piece of his victim's bloodstained shirt and walked away. He even had three teenage eyewitnesses, but once again, he easily avoided capture. He did send the shirt piece with a letter to the police.

His victims were all young people—between 16 and 29. And while these were verified Zodiac murders, there were others before and after these (including the murder of a police officer) that are suspected to be the work of this diabolic killer.

HIS LETTERS

What added to the tragic drama of the Zodiac killing episodes was the letters he sent out to the police department and the newspapers—full of mystery, threat and a fair amount of cry for attention. The mystery was in the cryptic messages that he claimed held the answer to his identity—till date, only one of the four have been solved.

The threat was in his demand for his cryptograms to be published in the papers, or else he would 'cruise around all weekend killing lone people in the night, then move on to kill again'! He used to keep count of his victims in the various letters he sent out, and his final letter concluded with 'Me = 37, SFPD = 0', taunting the San Francisco Police Department.

THE SUSPECTS

One man. 37 claimed murders. Around 2,500 suspects.

Yes! The failure to have caught the real Zodiac Killer definitely cannot be due to lack of trying. Over the years, there have been thousands of suspects. One, however, stood out more sharply than the others.

This person was Arthur Leigh Allen. Discharged from the US Navy, he was the major suspect since the beginning of the investigations. A convicted man, his friend informed the police about their conversations before the murders even started, wherein Allen spoke of wanting to kill people and calling himself the Zodiac. The Zodiac typewritten letters were created with a typewriter whose exact model was found in Allen's house as well. However, since the DNA found outside the stamps of the letters' envelopes and also the handwriting did not match, he was never convicted. However, it is believed that the DNA from under the stamp that the killer would have licked might match Allen's.

> **THE COLLECTOR OF SLAVES**
>
> The only Zodiac cryptogram that was solved revealed that he was killing people to collect slaves for his afterlife when he would be reborn in paradise! And it was not the police who solved it, but two regular citizens!

> **THE ZODIAC IN POP CULTURE**
>
> The first movie about the mass murderer was *The Zodiac Killer*, released in 1971, when he was still on the loose. The latest movie directly about him was *Zodiac* (2007), directed by David Fincher of *Gone Girl* fame.

There were many others. People used to ring up the SFPD offering names of supposed suspects. Even as the case started getting cold, they would still get around four calls monthly—mostly from amateurs eager to put forth their latest hypotheses.

WHY IS HE STILL NOT CAUGHT?

Firstly, the files and evidences were very poorly maintained. In fact, as the case attained an almost mystical status, retired officers would apparently steal from the documents to keep as souvenirs!

Secondly, the internal politics and conflicts among the SFPD officials probably contributed a lot too. Even as late as 1999, two officers, Kelly Carroll and his partner Maloney, started reworking the case on the basis of DNA evidence—this was aired on TV and allegedly made their superior, John Hennessy, jealous. There were other factors involved as well, and before they could reach the end of their investigation, it was called off by Hennessy in 2004.

It has been picked up again in 2018 and if we are lucky, it won't be long before the identity of the maniacal Zodiac Killer ceases to be a cryptic mystery of American history.

51

The Curious Mystery of the Electric Girl

> *'The human body is strange and flawed and unpredictable. The human body has many secrets, and it does not divulge them to anyone, except those who have learned to wait.'*
>
> —Paul Auster

'If you had a superpower, what would you want it to be?' If you haven't been asked this fun question among friends, you're probably one of very few. Science fiction literature and comic books have pushed the limits of imagination when it comes to this—and continues to do so. And yet, actual incidents of display of superhuman powers lie buried deep within the pages of history. Let's take one of them out to bring to you—the electric girl.

WHO IS SHE?

It was a cold January day in 1846 when Angelique Cottin, a fourteen-year-old peasant girl in rural France started exhibiting signs of psychokinesis. It is a psychic ability that allows one to control objects without touching them. Cottin and some other girls were weaving silk gloves on a wooden frame when the frame began moving all of a sudden. It was only when they stepped away that the shaking stopped.

When they approached it, the frame again started moving only when Cottin came closer. It was the beginning of what was to be one of the strangest episodes in the history of reported psychokinesis.

Not surprisingly, the first guess everyone made about the cause of her condition was witchcraft. The local priest could come to no conclusions. But her family certainly did—they saw the possibilities of making money from her unnatural powers, and so promptly took her to Paris to allegedly put her on some sort of exhibition.

MAGNETIC MANIFESTATIONS

In the meanwhile, her condition started worsening as her powers continued to grow stronger. She couldn't sit on a chair without the chair pulling or pushing itself away; even a strong man couldn't hold the chair down when she was touching it. Beds would rock when she tried to sleep on them and other heavy furniture moved away at the slightest contact with her. And being near her would cause sudden electric shocks.

It was an odd type of erratic magnetic or electrical attraction, which would be lessened only if she was sitting on a carpet or waxed cloth. It would stop manifesting for a couple of days, and then start again.

A cold wind is supposedly felt during paranormal manifestations such as poltergeist hauntings. A similar drop in temperature was experienced by those near Cottin. Other abnormal physical traits she exhibited were being extreme sensitivity to stimuli, muscle convulsions, and an increased heart rate of 120 beats per minute. These episodes used to upset her terribly, causing her to run away from the scene. And the more tired she got, the weaker her powers would grow.

When it came to diagnosing and treating her, she was taken to a Dr Tanchau who conducted a number of tests on her, as did others after him. Being near a ball of feathers hung on a silk thread caused it to either be attracted towards or repelled away from her body. Compasses would move violently if placed near her. If she brought her left wrist near a burning candle, the flame would bend horizontally—as if someone was blowing on it continuously.

SINCERE OR SHAM

Dr Tanchau was convinced enough about the authenticity of Angelique's powers to bring in physicist and astronomer Francois Arago to witness the phenomenon. Arago too was impressed enough with the abnormal electromagnetism to set up an official committee to enquire into it formally.

While it seemed clear that the electric girl certainly possessed some powers of psychokinesis, there were critics who believed that she was cheating. They said she did so by pushing the small furniture from under her petticoat with a movement so swift that it was hard to detect. While this does not explain how she could cause bigger and heavier items such as dining tables to smash against walls, detractors also posit that these accounts could be heavily fabricated.

In any case, these unnatural manifestations stopped after four months, in April—but it is believed that she continued to fake them at the behest of her family so as to put on exhibitions in Paris to earn money.

Almost two centuries later, as we enjoy our X-Men and Avengers comics and movies, the real-life mystery of superhuman abilities becomes nothing but a trivia to discuss. If we could have found an answer to this, who knows—we could have perhaps delved deeper into the biggest mystery ever—the human mind.

> **MORE THAN ONE SUPERHUMAN**
>
> Not surprisingly, Cottin was not the only one in history to display such powers. Hovering between the spectrum of false claims and true accounts, there are a number of names that pop up, one of which is a Mademoiselle Emmerich. She reportedly had a frightful incident once, post which she fell into deep trauma and started exhibiting electromagnetic powers. She could transmit electric shocks to people near her without touching them, and this stopped only when she died.

Acknowledgements

Every night as I turned off my laptop after completing yet another bit of this book, two thoughts ran through my mind simultaneously—how writing a book is one of the hardest but most fulfilling things I will ever undertake and how lucky I am to have the support system I do in my life to be able to accomplish it. So, this acknowledgement should come easy, and yet I worry it will never be enough to express just how grateful I am to each and every person who made this happen.

The two people in the world on whose feet I forever lay my grateful heart are my parents, Moni Saikia and Jyoti Prova Changmai Saikia. From looking after their granddaughter while I worked from home during the day and worked on the manuscript at night, to being my source of comfort whenever things got too difficult—like they tend to get sometimes—this book would not have been possible without them.

I am eternally grateful to my younger sister, Bhaswati Saikia, for being my sounding board, my trustworthy confidante and another reliable babysitter to her niece. The late nights would not have been as zesty if I did not have her to pitch my thoughts to, every once in a while.

I am thankful to my husband Dibyendu Deb Roy, whose unwavering confidence in me was just the motivation I needed every step of the way to bring this project to light.

I am thankful to all my friends, whose constant enthusiasm for this work gave me the regular boost I needed to push myself just a little bit harder every time. I especially want to thank Rohini Deb, Rashee Mehra and Sahiba Sethi for their invaluable inputs right from the start and helpful advice throughout.

Most importantly, I want to thank my little girl, Dakshita Deb Roy (Zoe). The soul of this book has drunk deep from the wells of the child-like curiosity and fearless spirit of adventure that define her.

I am humbled to leave her this as my legacy, and hope that in the coming years she enjoys reading each chapter with as much thrill as I did when I wrote them.

www.ingramcontent.com/pod-product-compliance
Lightning Source LLC
Chambersburg PA
CBHW020231170426
43201CB00007B/386